T0279495

GENDERED ISLAMOPHOBIA

GENDERED ISLAMOPHOBIA
My Journey With a Scar(f)

MONIA MAZIGH

MAWEN*Z*I
HOUSE

We acknowledge the support of the Canada Council for the Arts for our publishing program. We also acknowledge support from the Government of Ontario through the Ontario Arts Council, and the support of the Government of Canada through the Canada Book Fund.

Cover design by Sabrina Pignataro
Cover photo: Mary Long / Five women of different ethnicities and cultures stand side by side together. Strong and brave girls support each other and feminist movement. Sisterhood and females friendship. Vector illustration / Shutterstock.com

Library and Archives Canada Cataloguing in Publication

Title: Gendered Islamophobia : my journey with a scar(f) / Monia Mazigh.
Names: Mazigh, Monia, author.
Description: Includes bibliographical references.

Identifiers: Canadiana (print) 20230210066 | Canadiana (ebook) 2023021021X | ISBN 9781774151037 (softcover) | ISBN 9781774151044 (EPUB) | ISBN 9781774151051 (PDF)

Subjects: LCSH: Mazigh, Monia. | LCSH: Muslim women—Canada—Biography. | LCSH: Muslim women—Canada—Social conditions. | LCSH: Women in Islam—Canada. | LCSH: Islamophobia. | LCGFT: Autobiographies.

Classification: LCC HQ1170 .M39 2023 | DDC 305.48/697092—dc23

Printed and bound in Canada by Coach House Printing

Mawenzi House Publishers Ltd.
39 Woburn Avenue (B)
Toronto, Ontario M5M 1K5
Canada

www.mawenzihouse.com

We heard the account of another child, a 7-year-old, whose name was also Osama. Sensing the backlash and the growing tide of intolerance, his teacher suggested that from now on he would be called Sam. We need Canadians to know that Osama is a Canadian name, that Mohammed is a Canadian name and that worshipping in a mosque is a Canadian tradition.

Alexa McDonough,
former leader of the New Democratic Party,
October 2, 2001, in the Canadian Parliament

Women are the ones receiving the most violence from Islamophobia.

Khaled A Beydoun, *American Islamophobia:
Understanding the Roots and Rise of Fear*

. . . It is our institutions that are responsible for creating and reinforcing biases and assumptions held by individual members of society about racialized groups. These biases fuel individuals' discriminatory behaviours against members of the group in their daily interactions.

Ibram X Kendi, *How to Be an Antiracist*

Contents

Introduction: Why English

This book has a complicated genesis. It was meant to be written in French. I grew up going to school in French and Arabic; I loved the French language, it shaped my imagination, my thinking, and my prose. My high school best friend's mother once observed that I must be knowing a lot about Paris just from my reading of Emile Zola's works. She was partly right. I could imagine the department stores of Second Empire Paris, described so meticulously in Zola's *Au bonheur des Dames*, and the old *Les Halles* market, which was at the centre of his *Le Ventre de Paris* I learned of Haussmann's metamorphosis of Paris from reading Zola. But I didn't visit Paris until some forty years later. When I did, I was no longer a teenage idealist. Many things had happened, both personal and political, that made me nervous about walking those grand boulevards. First the 9/11 attacks, then the arrest of my husband Maher Arar by the American authorities and his rendition to Syria to be tortured, and of course the attacks on Charlie Hebdo and the Bataclan Theatre. There was too much violence that involved me directly or indirectly because of my background.

Before my trip to Paris and its charged atmosphere, I had thought of replacing my hijab with a hat, because I felt certain that I would suffer abuse in the streets, those same streets that once had charged my imagination as I held a French book in my hands, lying in my bed in Tunis. But my visit turned out to be largely safe, though I was always self-conscious and aware of my actions and words. But once when I let my guard down, a small incident happened that bothered me a little. I was in the metro, where the entrance gate was so heavy that I forgot to hold it for the person behind me. It was a woman, and she mumbled an insult at me. A typical Parisian, some would say. What can you do? Perhaps she had had a bad day. But perhaps she was another Islamophobe, a hater of Muslims, who had picked on me because I was wearing a hijab. How could one tell? Hatred gives us a thin skin. Regardless of that incident, I was happy to be almost invisible in the streets and the undergrounds of Paris.

But that same invisibility followed me in *Le Salon du livre de Paris*.

The purpose of my visit to the *Salon* was to display two of my books—a novel, *Du pain et du jasmin*, and a memoir, *Hope and Despair*—in the Quebec-Canada booth at the Salon and hopefully to sell them. *Le Salon* is a huge event, where popular, celebrity authors are conspicuously visible. But it is not every day that a woman in hijab stands at a booth at a French book fair. Naïvely I assumed that people would be curious and stop to ask questions about me and my books. And so I waited and waited, smiled and smiled, until my time ran out. A few times I spotted some North African-looking women and got ready to chat with them, but they simply hastened their pace and disappeared from my sight. I was, essentially, invisible there.

And so, the positive invisibility in the Paris streets, where I didn't feel the glares of people or experience abuse, was replaced by a negative invisibility. The visibility I longed for was denied to me. When I really wanted the salon visitors to open their eyes to my presence as a Muslim woman writer presenting her books, they chose to look away.

This invisibility is another garment that I wear. But I didn't choose to wear it, it was forced upon me by selective eye gazes and reserved attitudes. I realized that for most people I existed only through media exposures, usually controversial and negative, or through their own prejudices. No matter what I did, whether I was active or passive, angry or calm, I would remain that frozen image they saw on television or had read about. An encounter with a real Muslim woman wearing a hijab didn't interest them, because they believed they already knew everything about me.

But what do they really know about me?

They think I am an oppressed woman. A popular journalist in Quebec once told me, before even debating with me, "It doesn't matter how many PhDs you hold [I hold two], with your hijab you remain for me an oppressed woman!" How did the hijab come to be perceived as a sign of oppression? According to this view, hiding a woman's hair is a sign of oppression while exposing her breasts in public is a sign of liberation. A Quebec Muslim woman teaching in a classroom in a hijab is seen as proselytizing and a threat to the *laïcité* of the state.

I had intended to write this book in French. But just before I began, in August 2016, the "burkini gate" fiasco happened in France. A photo in the news caught my attention. A Muslim woman in a burkini—a bathing suit consisting of leggings, a tunic, and a headscarf—was lying on a beach, most likely napping, when four police officers came over to demand that she remove her burkini. That picture felt like an act of violence on my own body. I could have been that woman. I grew up in Tunis by the Mediterranean Sea, across the water from that very beach in Nice, France, and I learned to swim from an early age. Later, I decided to swim in an outfit in which I would feel comfortable and at ease. I wouldn't have liked people staring at my body—at my thighs, my breasts, my stomach. Wearing a burkini was and is my wish. By wearing it I am not making a political statement about feminism or Islam or anything else. I am doing something I enjoy—swimming— while keeping my body unexposed.

The harrowing look captured on the face of that woman truly shocked me. I felt the aggression in my own body, felt the misogyny blowing in my face. I felt the experience of French colonialism crawling under my skin. And I was reminded of how in Mecca, Saudi Arabia, where once I went for a small pilgrimage with my late father, I was policed by both men and women, known as "morality agents" (*mutaween*), and commanded by them to stay in the women's prayer section, far away from my father, who needed my help, and to remove my camera.

Colonialism is an odd thing. It doesn't disappear with handshakes by well-intentioned (or not) leaders. It doesn't skip generations. It stays dormant and then it awakes. When it awakes, it takes—for example—the shape of four French police officers forcing a Muslim woman on a beach to remove her burkini. The humiliation of a Muslim woman on a beach having to decide between being French and being Muslim. And they say, "It is their men who impose on them what to wear"!

It might be argued that the police officers were simply enforcing "good morals and secularism," the exact words used by the officials. But the same could be said of those who "impose" hijab (or other policies) on women "to protect good morals and religion." Laïcité is simply a veil behind which the state may very well hide its racism and Islamophobia.

I didn't live through colonialism. My father did but he rarely told me stories about it. Rather, he sent me to a private school where I learned both Arabic and French. And I loved French. I grew up thinking that French was the language of great literature, of great philosophers, and great art and film. The language of Hugo, Zola, Sartre, and others that would enlighten me. But when I saw that woman forced to reveal her skin to prove her allegiance to the values of the *République*, I realized that my father didn't tell me all the stories about colonialism. He forgot to tell me the bad ones. He wanted me to learn French to be "civilized." He had internalized colonialism.

Obviously, by learning French, thinking in French, and loving the language, I still couldn't be properly, completely French by state standards. My burkini, like the burkini of that woman, was the first hurdle; then there was my faith. That is the power of colonialism. It judges you and puts you in your place.

And so, as an angry, impulsive, hysterical Muslim woman with a hijab, I decided to stand up to that colonizer. I didn't want to write this book in the language of those who were violating the physical and emotional integrity of a woman who could have been me.

I am not rejecting French. I am using my right to decide which language to use to speak about the violence that is being directed at Muslim women with hijab. Using French to speak about such a topic would be to acquiesce to the aggression.

Which language the former colonized people of the world should use has long been the subject of debate among writers. Kateb Yacine, a postcolonial Algerian author famously said, "I write in French to tell the French I am not French."[1]

Previous to this book my preference for French had prevailed over English. I had come to Quebec for my higher studies. When I was admitted to a PhD program at McGill University, I was seriously tempted to continue at my French business school, the *École des Hautes Études Commerciales de Montréal*, where I had completed my master's. I listened to the radio in French, I read in French. I had written one memoir and three novels in French. But for this book, I couldn't use French. It would be using the language of the oppressor to denounce the oppression, in a version of the Stockholm Syndrome.

Why English, the language of another colonialist power? English came to me through pop music, and later through academic papers, and later still through advocacy writing and political activism. I don't have an emotional connection with English. But it allows me to communicate highly polarized ideas, controversial opinions, and strong emotions. In my mind there was a power struggle between the message and the messenger. I wanted to keep an emotional distance from the messenger and give space to the message: this book.

An Urgent Calling

I began to write this book with an urgency because of the issues involved. I did not have a specific audience in mind. This is a personal book, and many times I thought of giving up writing it, because it could be seen as bitter, or cynical and angry, or at times "Quebec-bashing." But if I continued with it, I had to be true to myself and write what I believed with honesty and without fear.

I wrote this book as a Canadian Muslim woman. These are the three descriptions I carry with me, acquired by birth and by choice. I was born a girl in a Muslim country to Muslim parents. I was raised as a "cultural" Muslim. I practised without questioning. Islam was for me a series of cultural practices including many festivities, which were occasions to eat and be happy. Later my readings began to shape my choices and views. I read novels, poetry, history, and books on religion, in both Arabic and French, the languages that I loved. Reading Arabic, I learned to appreciate its vocabulary and rich semantics. It opened a window to my Islamic knowledge. In French I discovered new places and cultures that exercised my imagination.

Navigating the two worlds is exciting, but poses important questions What is my identity? Who am I? I spent much of my teenage years trying to answer these questions through books and loud discussions with my father and endless arguments with my friends. In my early twenties, I made my own decision to wear a headscarf and a few months later I decided to immigrate to Canada.

These two decisions seem to be choices. But are they really? I can remove the headscarf, never wear it again—except that it had become a part of me. It shaped me as much as I shaped its meaning.

The principal of the *Institut des Hautes Études Commerciales* in Tunis, where I was studying finance, called me for a meeting one day with two other young women who were also wearing the hijab. The principal informed us that very soon, we would not be allowed to enter the campus with the hijab on our heads. We looked at each other in shock and then one of the other girls replied: "I can't come to classes without my hijab. It is a part of me. It is exactly as if they asked you to come to school in your underwear and bra only. It would feel the same for me."

I and the other girl nodded in solidarity and to acknowledge the accuracy of that comparison. The principal was passively nodding, but she kept repeating the same new directive about banning hijab in all universities.

In Canada, I became the immigrant "woman with the headscarf," or the Muslim woman. I started my life in this new world, continuing to define myself and adding a new piece to my identity puzzle: what does it mean to be a Canadian?—until the attacks of 9/11 happened, after which I found myself dragged into the "war on terror." My hijab was now a sign of my "complicity" in the malefic forces that wanted to destroy Western civilization. No matter how distant I was from terrorism, two of my identities became de facto sources of guilt: Islam and the hijab.

On September 25, 2002, my husband, Maher Arar, boarded a plane from Tunis, my hometown where we had spent the summer with our two children. Maher's destination was Montreal. He never made it. He was detained on September 26, when he arrived at JFK airport in New York for a stopover. He was interrogated at length by FBI agents at the airport, after which he was transferred to the Metropolitan Detention Centre where he was strip-searched and kept incommunicado for weeks. In Tunisia, where I was with our two children, I waited impatiently for his phone call, increasingly worried and hoping that his silence could only be due to a missed flight. That phone call came more than a year later. He had been "rendered" on a plane from the US to Jordan, where he was again interrogated and then driven to Damascus,

Syria, his hometown, where he was kept imprisoned until his release on October 13, 2003. The American authorities alleged that he was "associated with Al-Qaeda." During that terrible ordeal, when he was tortured physically and mentally, he was never charged by any government. Needless to say, this tragic episode completely transformed all our lives—my husband's, mine, and my children's. We were never the same again.

But what has this to do with hijab, and writing this book? During my husband's disappearance, I became willy-nilly a public figure, the person who advocated on his behalf, his defender, his voice, which he had been robbed of. My public appearances and the public campaign I conducted for his release gave me a visibility I wasn't accustomed to. But it was another visibility, a negative sort, linked to terrorism in the post 9/11 world.

Many times, I had to defend my husband from allegations of terrorism that were thrown at him while implicitly defending myself from the stereotypes of a hijab-wearing Muslim woman. Was I just another Muslim wife who had been totally brainwashed by her husband? Could my husband have led a double life that I wasn't aware of? Even after he was released and Justice Dennis O'Connor, who conducted a lengthy public inquiry on the matter from 2004 to 2007, cleared his name from all terrorism allegations, my public persona was framed through a misogynistic lens: the wife of Maher Arar.

Despite the fact that I had lived in Montreal for many years and was fluent in French, my husband's case went almost unnoticed by the French media, until an investigative reporter, Brigitte Bureau from Radio-Canada in Ottawa, contacted me a few months before Maher's release and closely followed the case thereafter.

I attribute this quasi-invisibility of Maher's case to my hijab. The image of an educated Muslim woman who was wearing a hijab speaking for her husband's rights went against all the orientalist images popularized by media and politicians. Later, when a male journalist from Radio-Canada wrote a sympathetic piece about me in a Quebec newspaper, he mentioned that some people found the image of a Muslim woman wearing a hijab "aggressante."

I am not implying here that the media in Quebec is more

Islamophobic than the rest of Canada. I am saying that, for whatever reasons, the ordeal of my husband taken by me into the public space didn't gather as much interest in the Quebec French media as it did in the English media.

In 2006, the media and politicians of Quebec started a debate about "reasonable accommodation." As a francophone Muslim woman who had lived in the province of Quebec for many years, I felt rather drawn into the discussion. I followed the debate conscientiously, and at times I was invited to participate in interviews. The general atmosphere was not sympathetic to women wearing hijab, to say the least. During the years that followed, until today, legislations were introduced and made their way into the lawbooks of Quebec to ban religious symbols in some specific professions. Everybody agrees that the main religious symbol targeted was the hijab. Quebec is a distinct society. The proponents of such legislation have argued that equality between men and women as well as the province's *laïcité* ideal should be reflected in its laws. But as I have said, *laïcité* is a veil behind which governments and institutions may hide their Islamophobia. Quebec refuses the multiculturalism associated with the father and son Trudeau.

Once at a lunch with some of my French Canadian female colleagues, one of them who was recently separated from her partner happily announced that she had found a new *chum*, using an online platform. She candidly explained how she spent her first weekends at his place doing his laundry and that of his two teenage boys. I was shocked. Everyone laughed. But what if I had made a similar confession to my colleagues? Would they have laughed it off, taking it as a cute revelation? I found it shocking that a woman would find it normal to do the laundry of three men, just because she had moved in with one of them. It was unfair and demeaning. There is no law in Quebec that would protect women from being willingly humiliated in the house. But there is currently a law in Quebec that would prevent me, as a Muslim woman wearing a hijab, from teaching in public schools. No other province in Canada has similar legislation. Disagreeing with the current legislation in Quebec, rightly calling it Islamophobic is not Quebec-bashing.

Islamophobia exists in Canada everywhere. It exists in many

countries around the world. It even exists in Muslim countries. Consider these troubling statistics:[1]

» Two-in-five Canadians (39%) hold an unfavourable view of Islam. In Quebec that number reaches half (52%).

» 50% of Canadians think that Canada has a problem with Islamophobia and 50% think it does not. The same proportions are observed in Quebec.

» 25% of Canadians would support a law that would ban hijab. That supports climbs to 57% in Quebec.

» 67% of Canadians are comfortable with a mosque built in their neighbourhood. Only 53% are comfortable with that in Quebec.

» 52% of Canadians accept the idea that one of their children would marry a Muslim. Only 38% accept that idea in Quebec.

In this book, I will describe Islamophobia from a mainly personal point of view but also give academic sources for the term. Islamophobia isn't a new phenomenon, it existed before the 9/11 attacks. It appeared in movies, books, and media. However, I believe the attacks of 9/11 and the advent of the anti-terrorism legislations in many countries, like the Patriot Act in the US and the Anti-terrorism legislation in Canada, exacerbated hatred of Muslims. These events created a fertile ground for normalizing Islamophobia. Combined with the misogyny that still prevails in many aspects of our societies, Islamophobia makes Muslim women wearing a hijab an easy and obvious target.

My objective with this book is to share with the readers some of my experiences and reflections. I don't claim to represent all Muslim women. Perhaps some. Muslim women are diverse in their spirituality, in their understanding of the religious texts, in their languages and cultures, in their socioeconomic backgrounds, and in their sexual orientations.

I hope this book will help to humanize Muslim women. Following the footsteps of French philosopher Michel Montaigne, I deliver this essay as a testimony of my strengths and weaknesses as a Muslim Canadian woman. My ultimate objective is to foster understanding, empathy, and compassion. I dream of the day where despite our differences, we will be able to respect and accept each other.

What Is Islamophobia?

The first time I experienced what I would call Islamophobia in Canada was when I applied to McGill University for a PhD degree in finance. (My very first experience of this kind of discrimination was when I graduated from my university in Tunis, as I describe later.) It was in the spring of 1994, and I was about to complete my master's degree at the *École des Hautes Études Commerciales* in Montreal. My friends and professors had encouraged me to apply to an English university for a different experience in higher learning. Indeed, what was more prestigious than McGill University? I applied there and waited. Then one day quite randomly I met a friend of mine on the street. She was also from Tunisia. We had gone to the same business school there. She was a good student and one year ahead of me. She had come to Canada as an international student, and I as a landed immigrant. She was doing a master's in international business. Our paths were almost identical, and she had also applied to McGill to the PhD finance program. The only obvious difference between us was that I wore a headscarf and she didn't.

She was excited that day and told me that she had received an acceptance letter from McGill and most likely would accept the offer. "How about you?" she asked me. "Not yet," I replied. I thought the letter might be in my mailbox. There was nothing when I checked. Two days later I received a letter informing me that I wasn't accepted because there were many good candidates, and I was on a waiting list.

Why was it a no for me and a yes for her, I kept asking myself. Given our almost identical academic backgrounds, the only explanation I can think of is my hijab, the headscarf. It scares people; it makes them uneasy. It makes me feel unwelcome. I called the secretary of the program at McGill. I was blunt. "Why wasn't I accepted whereas my friend was?" She didn't have a reply but promised to let the director of the program know of my concern. A few days later, a letter arrived in the mail, informing me that I had been "boosted" in the waiting list and that there might be some cancelations soon. Even better, the same day I received a personal phone call from the director to tell me that I had been accepted in the program. I felt that this incident could have only one plausible explanation: my hijab or whatever it represented to some people. I had been rejected because of it. It seems to me that only when I had raised the issue of discrimination was I treated fairly and the previous decision overturned. There is no absolute proof, of course, but for me it is the first serious episode of Islamophobia that I encountered in Canada. Years later, when I recall it, I am still shocked. I had believed that Canada was different from Tunisia, that my hijab would not be a source of exclusion. The years have shown me over and over that I was wrong.

Asking you to define something that you have been experiencing and know well can be a daunting task. It is like asking you to define what it means to be a woman or what it means to be a child. The difficulty doesn't come only from the fact that you live in it and with it daily and lack the proper words to explain it to others who do not live it, but also from the fact that all our relationships as humans are influenced by power. A child may not be able explain her frustrations when an adult doesn't understand her. This is mainly because the child can't translate emotions into words, but also because the child and the adult have different realities, different understandings of the world they live in; on top of that, there is always the power relationship between the child and the adult, who can be a parent, a caregiver, a teacher, etc. This particular relationship shapes the words to describe the child's experiences and perspectives—being misunderstood, abused, and so on.

Similarly, how can a woman explain how she feels to a man? This explanation would depend on the relationship she has with the man. If there is friendship, one of the parties might make more effort to understand the other. If there is love, the explanation given by the woman will depend on the readiness of the man to accept and embrace his partner's versions of her experiences. However, if there is a clear power relationship like in a labour context or a family or an organization such as the workplace, the woman's feelings would be either seriously accepted, dismissed, or mocked.

With Islamophobia, asking the question itself can be a sign of denying it, or doubting its existence as a phenomenon, or doubting the credibility of the person talking about it.

Often, I have found myself trying to explain Islamophobia to people who are not Muslims, and their reactions ranged from incredulity, to incomprehension, to acknowledgement, to minimizing it, to justifying it, or to flatly denying it. Those reactions are undoubtedly linked to my persona and to the kind of relationships I have with my interlocutors. For some, as a Muslim woman wearing a headscarf I could be suspected of a hidden agenda, i.e. of exaggerating isolated or innocuous incidents in order to feel victimized and gain sympathy. For others, my hijab and my obvious religious identity would render my testimony, coming from a truth bearer, unquestionable and forceful. For still others, I could be spreading false news to protect "my own people" and downplay legitimate criticism about Islam or Muslims.

And so my physical appearance and the visibility of my faith would always tip the balance of any argument for me or against me— my objectivity was lost the minute I put a headscarf over my head. Therefore, instead of fighting these misperceptions, I will openly be subjective and remain true to my feelings.

In this book, therefore, dealing about a subject that is close to me, I will have two perspectives: a very personal one that could be accused of being biased or emotional and carrying a hidden agenda, but which I consider relevant, genuine, and crucial; and an objective one that is academic and will refer to studies and reports, enough to reassure or nullify the cynics.

In the Runnymede Trust's report, *Islamophobia: A Challenge for Us All* (1997), Islamophobia is defined as an outlook or worldview involving an unfounded dread and dislike of Muslims, resulting in practices of exclusion and discrimination.

In another report, *Berkeley University: Islamophobia Research and Documentation Project* (2013), Islamophobia is defined as a contrived fear or prejudice fomented by the existing Eurocentric and Orientalist global power structure. It is directed at a perceived or real Muslim threat through the maintenance and extension of existing disparities in economic, political, social, and cultural relations, while rationalizing the necessity to deploy violence as a tool to achieve "civilizational rehab" of the target communities (Muslim or otherwise). Kanji et al (2017) define Islamophobia as unfounded or irrational fear and/or hatred of Islam or Muslims (or people perceived to be Muslims), leading to violence and systemic discrimination. Semantically speaking, the word "Islamophobia" is controversial in the sense that some claim that it is a new word and in consequence this shows that Islamophobia is a new construct merely intended to "silence" the critics of Islam.

The word *Islamophobia* or rather the French term *islamophobie* seems to have been first coined and introduced by Alphonse-Étienne Dinet, a French orientalist painter in his 1922 essay, "L'Orient vu de l'Occident." Dinet lived in Algeria, where he painted Algerian subjects, learned Arabic, and translated several books from Arabic into French. Later, he converted to Islam and became known as Nasreddine Dinet. Thus the word *Islamophobia* has been in use for some decades, but the recognition of the phenomenon it describes has been difficult. The refusal to accept the term as legitimate is in itself an indication of the intensity of the debate and the stubborn belief that since the word is not legitimate the phenomenon isn't either.

Applying the above definitions of Islamophobia, I can only conclude that my application for admission to McGill University had evoked an Islamophobic reaction, which was a rejection. There was nothing wrong with my application, it was as good in its content and strength as that of my friend, who had applied with me and been accepted; we are very similar in our ages, gender, nationality (Tunisians living in Canada), religion, and academic records. And so, I attribute McGill's first refusal of my application to my physical appearance and thus to the hijab that covers my head.

There is always the possibility that the initial silence (understood by me as a refusal), followed by my inclusion in the waiting list, then a quick acceptance by phone, may have been the result of a botched treatment of my application. But there was never a reference to any technical or human mistake by the institution. This could be dismissed as an unfortunate incident. It might even be argued that the incident doesn't really show any fear of Islam, Muslims, or Islamic symbols, but rather it indicates the presence of incompetent people who didn't assess my file seriously and professionally. This is exactly where the personal narrative enters. This is where my subjectivity makes sense: "Believe the victim." "Believe her."

First and foremost, I felt deeply that my particular treatment was linked to my obvious religious identity. Whether on purpose or randomly (I can't prove the systemic aspect of discrimination here), whether an innocent mistake or a systemic one, I was singled out. On the surface, there was no Islamophobia, since my friend, who is a Muslim, was accepted. But I chose to make my faith visible. I was simply being "me," and this is what led some people to "push my application aside," and render me "invisible." My hijab led to an unfounded or irrational fear and or hatred of Islam or Muslims; this led to my exclusion, which defines Islamophobia.

If my friend hadn't applied for the same program at the same time or that she hadn't been accepted, I would never have known why I was put on the waiting list. I would have probably accepted that there was an issue with my application. I would have blamed myself for not being good enough. If I hadn't picked up the phone and asked the administration why they had accepted my friend and not me, I would have probably convinced myself that being on the waiting list was good enough, a sort of better than nothing!

However, after I spoke out and put my finger on the injustice (as I perceived it), the situation was quickly corrected. The obvious was too big to be denied or hidden.

Islamophobia is insidious, hidden under many layers. You may never know what exactly happened in the mind of the person or persons who took that initial decision to put my application aside. Was it motivated by some irrational fear? Was it the fear to be associated with what the hijab is perceived to represent: extremism or oppression? Or was it simply incompetence and ignorance on the part of those making the decision? We rarely hear from those who are on the supply chain of Islamophobia. That is why it is crucial to hear from the ones who are on the receiving side; why it is important that everyone hears these stories. Not to rub it into their faces but to create awareness and fight Islamophobia together.

My intention isn't to impose my religious views on anyone. My intention is to be able to be practice my religion while achieving my dreams. How can this be a threat to anyone?

I think I was lucky. The fact that two young women with similar academic backgrounds applied the same year to the same academic institution and one got accepted immediately and the other was put on a "waiting list," doesn't happen every day. But it happened. And it happened to me. It was an eye-opener. But maybe this luck comes with a price. The price of carrying it with me for years to the point of sitting down one day and documenting what a statistically rare incident means in the life of a Muslim woman wearing a hijab.

Why I Wear a Hijab

I wasn't born wearing a hijab. I started wearing it at the age of twenty in the summer of 1990 in Tunis. I remember the look on my father's face when I told him I was going downtown to buy some fabric so my mother, a professional seamstress, would make me new pants, knee-length tunics, and headscarves. Why? he asked. I replied that this was how I wanted to go out. He said nothing. Never before had my father had an opinion on how I dressed. Calling him a liberal wouldn't be true. He was quite religious but never imposed his beliefs on my mother or my brother and me. A few times after I started wearing the hijab, he tried to convince me that my appearance with a headscarf was very traditional and conservative, but I pretended not to listen, and it stopped there.

I grew up in the 1970s in a middle-class family. My father was a public servant, a free spirit and an eternally opposing voice to Presidents Habib Bourguiba and later Ben Ali. He would openly criticize the policies of these presidents, which would make his friends and our relatives rather uncomfortable, but he never belonged to any party, political or religious. Today with hindsight I realize that the regime probably never found him dangerous and therefore he was tolerated.

My mother worked in the clothing industry for a few years before opening a small tailor shop in our garage, where she received her clients. Only one thing really mattered for my father: my brother's and my education. I remember how early every morning, my father and I waited for the bus to take us from our suburban home to my primary school. Sometimes we got a ride from a neighbour or an acquaintance who would drop us near the school on his way to work.

My father had decided to put my brother and me in a private school so that we could receive a good education in both French and Arabic. Public schools were crowded and not of high standard, according to my father. My school was named Jeanne D'arc (Joan of Arc) and was run by the congregation of the Sisters of Saint Joseph. The teachers were assorted Catholic nuns of French, Italian, Maltese, and Egyptian origin as well as Tunisian Muslims. It was an all-girls school with a big yard, spacious classrooms, and a large hall that was used for year-end celebrations and as a schoolyard on rainy days. There was a large garden in the grounds, where we played games and looked for turtles behind the trees, though I don't recall finding any. The school also had a chapel, where the sisters prayed and meditated. We could see the big bell of the chapel from the garden where we played. The education we received was secular, though most of the sisters wore a cap that covered their hair. Later some of them dropped the cap and kept their hair very short. For subjects in Arabic, like language, science, and mathematics, we were taught the same curriculum as the public schools. We even had civic and religious studies, exactly what other students learned in the public schools. For subjects in French, like reading, writing and grammar, we followed books that were used in the French school system. We started learning French in kindergarten whereas in public schools kids were introduced to French only in grade four.

Learning French properly was a ticket to a better education and good jobs. Since the independence of the country in 1956, it has been the francophone elite that has formed the establishment, including the top bureaucrats and the political class. My father had studied in both Arabic and French. I grew up reading my French and Arabic composition drafts to him, when he would nod in approval or shake his head to show disagreement. His intellectual approval and support meant a lot to me.

My mother hadn't pushed me to wear the hijab. She herself did not wear the hijab at the time. When I was thirteen, I came to her one day and told her, "I have decided: I am going to be a full-time Muslim. I

19

am going to wear a headscarf." She thought I was joking. "Are you serious?" she asked. She insisted that I was too young and constantly changing my opinions. "Wearing a headscarf is a big decision, why do you want to wear it while you are only thirteen?"

At that time, I used to wish my mother was "cool." I wished she would tell me, "Monia, you rock, go ahead and do whatever you wish!" Still, her response made me nervous. I asked myself what my friends in school would think of me. That I was an old-fashioned, weird teenager? Would they want to be my friends anymore? I wanted to be one of them. Wearing a headscarf, praying five times a day, and not going out with boys weren't the best ways to fit in at the time. I decided to postpone wearing a hijab.

I was never a girly girl. I didn't know how to put on makeup. I didn't know how to prepare sugar paste to remove hair from my legs and underarms. I didn't know how to flirt with boys. When, rarely, I put kohl in my eyes, I was so self-conscious I felt that everyone was looking at me. As a teenager, I rarely wore dresses or skirts. I was constantly in jeans and sneakers, and I hated how my hair looked. But I wasn't a social outcast. I had friends, I was very talkative (I am, still) and had strong political opinions. Being a girl like me in Tunisia in the 1980s was problematic. Girls were supposed to be girls. What made things even worse for me was my new, strong sense of religiosity. I prayed regularly and read all sorts of books, in Arabic, French, and later English. The books were mostly literary but sometimes about religion. Those two aspects of me were "abnormalities." They made me unplaceable. I didn't fit any of the boxes that our society had prepared for me.

I didn't fit into the "girly-girl" group, conforming to the social expectations of a woman, wearing makeup, straightening her hair, revealing her physical charms to attract prospective husbands. At the same time, I didn't fit the "liberal" box. I was not an atheist or agnostic or nonpracticing, like many liberal educated women were. My attachment to both religion and spirituality didn't conform to the way they lived. I could have easily rejected religion. My father prayed but didn't force me to pray. My mother was traditional, but prayers remained a personal matter for her. She never asked me to pray. Many of my friends were born in such families. But unlike them I had become religious. More and more I sought to learn about Islam, its philosophy and history, and to grow spiritually.

I enjoyed praying. Growing up, I remember sometimes going with my father to our mosque for the Friday prayer, a congregation prayer mandatory for Muslim men but optional for Muslim women. I loved mosques. Their calmness brought me a feeling of serenity. I would usually have brought a headscarf and long dress in a plastic bag, and I would quickly put them on once we had entered the praying area. I would sit near my father in the men's section. I never liked the women's section, where I felt self-conscious and aware of the older women staring at me. I must have been nine or ten when a man came up to my father and told him to ask his daughter to go to the women's section. Since then, gradually I stopped going to mosque; it had become complicated, and my studies also kept me busy. However, prayer remained an important part of my life. It eased my social and academic insecurities and gave me moral strength. It helped me understand why I was born, why I was born a girl, why my parents were the ones I was born to, and why I was born in that particular part of the world. It helped me understand what would happen to me after I died and therefore gave a meaning to my life. Speaking to Allah helped me answer impossible questions. But that meant, once again, that I was "outboxed."

Edward Said, speaking about his mixed name, his childhood, and his identity as an Arab Christian Palestinian who later lived in the United States wrote in his memoir "The travails of bearing such a name were compounded by an equally unsettling quandary when it came to language. I have never known what language I spoke first, Arabic or English, or which one was really mine beyond any doubt." Said called his memoir *Out of Place*. I've also always felt out of place, physically and intellectually.

Until the age of twenty, I was deeply religious but would also go to the beach and wear a swimsuit. Thus, I was an "invisible" Muslim. I would listen to my best friend telling me about her teenage love adventures, but would never allow myself to have a boyfriend. Not because I was fearful of my parents, but because I firmly believed that sexuality is appropriate and should be enjoyed within the framework of marriage. I listened to Western pop music and watched Western films and I loved dancing with my friends. I would read publications in French, from France and the Middle East, but also spent many hours reading Arabic and religious texts. I faced a constant dilemma. How could I reconcile my spiritual life with my worldly and material needs, such as being attractive to boys, shopping for clothes and other items, or going to the beach? How could I live in an environment where the practice of religion was all right for older people and for the disadvantaged and poor classes, whereas the bourgeois class I belonged to would only accept the modern liberal me without my spirituality?

For eight years, until I was twenty, I struggled to fit into the first, materialistic box. I had deferred wearing a hijab, though I was convinced that one day I would wear it; I couldn't say when. And so, I continued to pretend that I was a modern Tunisian Muslim, with religion not foremost on my mind. A Muslim who wore Western-style clothes, including a swimsuit at the beach, while at the same time I continued to pray five times a day. Almost no one among my friends prayed. Few of them fasted during Ramadan, the tenth month of the lunar calendar where body-abled Muslims abstained from food and water from dawn to dusk. They were "cultural" Muslims. That doesn't mean that they were bad Muslims. They were my friends and family. I grew up with them, I liked them and shared my life with them, but they also hindered my spiritual journey. With them I always had to hide my religiosity. And so, for years I squished myself into that modern liberal box until I decided it didn't fit me anymore.

Being a spiritual person in Tunisia in those times, was like being gay there today. "Coming out" was the most difficult decision that one faced. This was worse for girls than for boys.

I graduated top in my business school for which I was to receive an award. The ceremony took place in Carthage, near the Presidential Palace at the city hall. The laureates were from primary to university level, and the hall was crowded with parents and students. I went with my father and wore a knee-long tunic and a green headscarf, both made by my mother. She didn't come, because she was busy with work. My father was beaming all the time, standing at the entrance, and I sat in one of the rows reserved for the awardees. At some point a man came to me and asked for my name. "Monia Mazigh," I replied enthusiastically. He was holding a paper in his hands. I thought he was checking the names of all the recipients, but why had he singled me out? I didn't think more about it as I waited in the sweltering heat inside the hall.

I had always loved school. I worked hard and was always among the top students. I think my whole identity as a girl and a young woman was built around succeeding in school and being among the best. Receiving an award after four years of hard work was the best thing I could have imagined for me. My business school was one of the best in Tunis and the department of finance was prestigious.

My first two years at my business schools were hard. The school was far from my home, and I had to take a bus and a train to reach it. Public transportation wasn't very reliable, and sometimes I had to wait for an hour with my friends to catch a bus home. The trains were usually better in terms of timing, but they were crammed. Studying finance in Tunis in the early 1990s was a sort of an oxymoron. I remember one of my finance professors, a fresh graduate from the Paris Dauphine, the prestigious Parisian business school, telling us half jokingly, half mockingly that we should start reading the *Financial Times* since we were really "financially culturally illiterate."

He had a point. We studied finance, but only in theory. We had never heard of stock markets, our parents weren't stockholders, la bourse des valeurs mobilières de Tunis (The Tunisian stock exchange) was an unknown entity to most of us. The finance we knew and were familiar with was corporate finance, dealing with budgets, debt, and treasury management. Introducing us to concepts like financial markets, derivative products, risk management, and currency products created some sort of a cognitive dissonance. But we relied on reading and hard work to understand these concepts and yes, soon enough we started going to the newspaper stalls that used to fill the Habib Bourguiba sidewalks and share the cost of buying the recommended pink-coloured *Post*.

When I graduated top in my class, I felt proud and happy. But that hot day, as I waited in anticipation, my name was never called out. I looked desperately at all the kids being called out around me—the girl beside me, all the students in front me, and those behind rose and walked up to the stage. All of them stiff in their best clothes, showing their best smiles, hugging their parents afterwards and posing for the cameras. I was the only one left out. I was the only one in a hijab. All the others were "normally" dressed, I wasn't.

When the proceedings came to an end, I went to find my father who was standing by the door. "They didn't call me!" I cried out, holding back my tears. I could tell he was disappointed. We walked back to the train station and then waited for the bus. We got off and were a few blocks away from our house, when my father finally told me, "I think you should have dressed differently." I snapped back, "What do you mean?" My father hesitated then said, "Something modern, maybe without the headscarf, or some sort of a turban . . . As you were dressed, you looked so . . . so . . . serious, so religious . . . "

I didn't want to reply. I was crying. That was the last time my father made a comment on my attire. Years later, he would always have a compliment for me: "This long skirt looks nice on you." He was bitter that day because I didn't get my award. I was devastated. The man who had asked me for my name wasn't innocently checking my identity, he wanted my name to be crossed out from the list. Perhaps some city official in charge of the ceremony saw me and decided that my attire wasn't suitable and my presence as an award recipient shouldn't be publicly celebrated.

In Tunisia, a former French colony, a successful and liberated woman has only one image: that of a woman wearing Western-style clothing and free hair. I didn't fit that box. Despite my obvious academic abilities, I didn't fit. Where did this image originate? Who decides what a woman should wear? And why are certain clothes deemed liberating and others oppressive?

Personally, I found that the requirements on what to wear and what not to wear, what to reveal and what not to reveal of our bodies, and how to style our hair, restricting and intrusive, not to say oppressive. The hijab, as I understand it, as do many Muslim women worldwide, is liberating—as counterintuitive this may sound in the West. One is not judged on looks or body, one is not conscious of being on display— for sale, as it were. The Islamic notion of hijab is found in the Quran, believed by Muslims to be the word of God sent to his last messenger, the Prophet Muhammad, through the archangel Gabriel.

The notion of hijab in Islam isn't an instruction from a man, Prophet Muhammad, to the believers. It is a recommendation from God to His believers. God in the Islamic tradition is not a gendered entity. God is not a man or a woman. (I use my pronouns for God neutrally, not to indicate gender.) God is beyond any binary system of gender that has been traditionally accepted by many societies. In one of its best self-descriptions in the Quran, God calls Himself "Light upon Light."

I found liberation in hijab because I stopped caring about how to please my mother, my neighbour, my teacher, the policeman on the street or the politician trying to make gains at the expense of women's rights. I decided to please the Divine, to be above people's requirements, and instead to listen to God, the Light. I see the hijab as a personal covenant between my soul and my body. By deciding to wear the hijab, I was responding to a directive that I believed to be from God.

In the Quran, God, speaking to Prophet Muhammad, starts with the men, recommending them to be modest:

> Say to the believing men that they should lower their gaze and guard their modesty: that will make for greater purity for them: And Allah is well acquainted with all that they do. (The Holy Quran 24:30)

Moving on to women, God said:

> And say to the believing women that they should lower their gaze and guard their modesty; that they should not display their beauty and ornaments except what (must ordinarily) appear thereof; that they should draw their veils over their bosoms and not display their beauty except to their husbands, [a list of relatives], [household servants], or small children who have no sense of the shame of sex; and that they should not strike their feet in order to draw attention to their hidden ornaments. And O ye Believers! turn ye all together towards Allah, that ye may attain Bliss. (The Holy Quran 24:31)

25

In public, I keep my hair and some parts of my body covered. At home, I am free to wear what I wish and uncover my hair in front of my female friends and relatives and some of my male relatives like my father, my brother, and my uncles. This covenant is clear for me. There is a certain logic in it. For some it is archaic and constraining. For me, it works fine.

My acceptance of this reasoning doesn't make me less smart, oppressed, or a fanatic. It makes me a better human being. A woman who is in constant quest for harmony between her soul and her body.

The majority of Muslim scholars have interpreted the second verse above as a recommendation for women to cover their hair with a "khimar." It is the word used in the Quran to refer to the headscarf used by women at the time of the Prophet. When Muslim women pray, they cover their heads. When they are on the Pilgrimage, they cover their heads. When they enter a mosque, they cover their heads. It is a sign of respect and awareness of God's presence. I subscribe to this particular interpretation. I want to be constantly reminded of God's presence in my life. Hijab has helped me in that regard. I am filled with a sense of coherence: my physical appearance isn't in contradiction with my spiritual ideals.

Nevertheless, it is always important to remind myself and my readers that the hijab doesn't make of me a saint, free of sins. It doesn't make me spiritually superior to other women or Muslim women who do not wear hijab. The verses speak to me personally. The way I chose to cover my head and dress modestly helped me navigate through conflicting needs: my gender, my spiritual being, social expectations, physical desires, sexual needs, and cultural standards. The hijab helps me switch from the public to the private and put boundaries between the "friends" and the "foreigners"—those I accept in my private circle and those I keep in my public sphere.

Since my teenage years, when I became interested in the Islamic concept of hijab, until today, I have seen opinions from Muslims and non-Muslims that are against it. Most of them insist that the requirement of the hijab for women is either an old misogynistic interpretation of the Quran or an agenda of political Islamic groups.

I don't pretend to hold the Truth. I don't think that my choice is necessarily the best one. But I believe that my choice is right for me. My reflection on the hijab here is to help others understand why I wore the hijab and to expose the phenomenon of how women who wear it are subject to misunderstanding, discrimination, and Islamophobia. My intention is not to proselytize. Many people would disagree with my religious choice; that is expected. Purposely discriminating against women with hijab and using laws to ban it is wrong and incompatible with the tradition of liberal democracy that we are continuing to build and promote. Verbal abuse of Muslim women wearing a hijab should be seriously condemned. Physical attacks should be considered a hate crime.

The hijab can have several meanings, of course. It disturbs and scares some. It is seen as a tool of oppression, and indeed it can become one if a woman is coerced to wear one, just as anything else that is coerced. It has sometimes become a simple outfit for fashion. It can hide hair that we don't like. Or it is a shelter against wind and storm. Each woman has her own truth.

For centuries, the hijab worn by women represented the segregation between men and women and justified misogyny and oppression towards women. This segregation was often also present in Indian and European societies. In the last few decades of the twentieth century, the hijab became a tool for some Muslim women in patriarchal societies to regain their freedom from cultural norms designed to exclude them. At the same time it allowed generations of Muslim women to reclaim their feminism and their religious identities. For me it became something to ease my insecurities as a young woman thrown under the hegemony of the fashion and beauty industries on one hand and social norms on the other. It also became a tool for making peace with my spirituality, that is, accepting God in my life with no shame. That is why at the age of twenty, I decided to get out of the box and embrace my religious identity wholeheartedly. I became a "visible" Muslim woman, a muhajaba or what some call today a hijabi.

But I was breaking free from a box to unwillingly enter another one.

Hijab, Islam, and Other Religions

For some people, the requirement of the hijab, as invoked and described in the Quran, is unclear; the argument is that it was restricted to the wives of Prophet Muhammad and only limited to covering the bosom and the neck of women and not the hair; it was adopted later by traditional and conservative societies. I have heard and read many of these critics, Muslims and Non-Muslims, men and women, make their arguments against the hijab in modern life, but I do not believe their views to be absolutely valid or true.

I have read the Quran since I was a child. I have read the Surahs where the notion of hijab is mentioned. I have read them over and over. I have also read literal interpretations of the Quran, written mainly by male scholars. I have also read the reformist and more liberal interpretations of the verses, also written by mostly male and some female scholars. And I have made my choice.

In the words of God, I found liberation. Some would wonder how you can find liberation in a dogma. Isn't a belief a sort of a submission? Isn't a belief a way to lose one's rationale and become a prisoner of an ideology?

But can't we say the same thing about any other ideology—capitalism or socialism, or humanist? In a capitalist society we choose to wear clothes packaged for us and sold to us innocent consumers as simply belonging to the fashion of the day. Why are clothes that expose female bodies (rarely male bodies) seen as coming from free choice and why not the hijab? Why don't we simply accept that there is a wide range of beliefs and choices in our society and that openness and acceptance are a sign of progress towards real democracy free of discrimination?

A possible answer could be found in the understanding of religion in our society, and in particular the depiction of Islam. Religion has been demonized by many modern societies, especially those that were oppressed for centuries under the name of religion.

In Quebec, for instance, religion—the Catholic Church, and its institutions—dominated society since the arrival of the French settlers to the shores of the Saint Lawrence River. The Sisters of the Charité built hospitals and cared for the poor, and the monasteries trained the priests and much of the elite of the new French society. The priests organized the lives of men and particularly of women in all the villages of La Nouvelle France. Women suffered from poverty, lack of education, and the strict rules of the Church that dictated their personal lives. Their poverty, their ignorance, and their oppression were all explained and justified by the Church. The domination of the Catholic Church in Quebec remained until the Révolution tranquille of the 1960s.

Women's rights in Quebec became equivalent to women's liberation from the Catholic Church and thus from any religion. All the other religions came to be viewed through the prism of the Catholic Church. This fear or suspicion of the Catholic Church translated into fear of and suspicion of Islam when Muslims started to be more and more visible in the Canadian public space.

I am not saying that Islam is "better" than other religions. I am not an apologist for any religion. Religions and worship of a deity have always been part of human societies, and they have played crucial roles in shaping what we are today. Many wars were justified through claims of the supremacy of one religion over another. Millions of people have given their lives defending their religion. Even today, religion is still used by some as legitimate cause for killing. I denounce all forms of abuse and violence justified by religious interpretations, whether Christian, Judaist, Muslim, or any other. I believe that we cannot be governed by fear and violence, whether from a religious entity or a secular one. And we should not prevent women from displaying religious symbols, claiming that we know better than them.

The Islamic past is filled with incidents of violence and misogyny towards women. Two of my paternal aunts were deprived of their inheritances simply because they were women. Their siblings, my paternal grandfather and his brother, constantly squabbled over their family wealth, but when it came to their sisters' shares, they both agreed that the women didn't need as much as them since they were married; the two brothers therefore decided what their sisters received. This is not Islam. This is patriarchy, misogyny, and abuse.

Of course, Islam will always be used as a pretext to give less rights to women and to control their lives. The hijab became part of this system of oppression.

By removing hijab, oppression can't simply disappear. Conversely, by wearing it, one is not automatically oppressed. Oppression is deeply rooted in men's and women's minds. Dismantling oppression doesn't equate forcing women to remove their hijab. None of my older relatives, men or women, were particularly religious. Their acts were not motivated by any particular sense of devotion to God. My grandfather and his brother abused their sisters. The veneer of religiosity and conservatism that painted their society gave them the perfect excuse.

This being said, every religion has a liberating aspect or at least aspires to it. When it comes to Islam, this bright side is no exception. The hijab can imply oppression, but it can also imply liberation as I understood it and as many other women did when they decided to opt for the headscarf against the will of their mothers and fathers. This seeming contradiction has almost been wiped out of the public debate. You can either be pro hijab or against. Many times, in debates about women and Islam, I feel that the conversation is being conducted through a homogenizing prism. Journalists and commentators mostly repeat the same old stereotypes—backwardness and oppression—without any knowledge or understanding.

Many Muslim societies until today have been highly patriarchal and many aspects of women's oppression in Islamic countries have roots that go even deeper, to the times before the advent of Islam. The Quran didn't establish misogyny. Sometimes it tried to break it, as in the strong and clear condemnation of femicide, a practice that predated

Islam. In other circumstances, the Quranic message tried to tame long-held misogyny, for example by allowing women to have their share of inheritance (they were excluded before), even if that share wasn't always equal to that of their male counterparts. In other passages, the Quranic message accepted the patriarchal model by giving men more power over women in the framework of marriage, when it allowed admonishing them or correcting them. (We should not forget that in European societies of the time women were mere possessions of the men, and until very recently husbands were allowed legally to beat their wives.)

The Quran is not exempt from reformist interpretations. There are already many new readings of the Quran with feminist, liberal, and radical approaches. This richness of views and approaches is rarely discussed in the media, both in Muslim and non-Muslim countries.

Despite the existence of some crucial differences between Islam and other religions, and despite the diversity of opinions within Islam, it is unfortunate that many debates conducted in the media about Islam or matters affecting Muslim women often exclude Muslim women and are dominated by the misleading vision that women are inherently oppressed in Islam. My main argument here is that matters that affect Muslim women are most of the time examined through the distorted and sometimes biased lenses of other religions or in the absence of diverse interpretations and opinions. This is what I call the "homogenization project."

The minute you call yourself a Muslim or you look like a Muslim woman, you are judged by principles that do not hold true even in Islam. Worse, when Muslim women's views are brought into the discussion, they are usually chosen to regurgitate the same narratives already existent about them. Many of these voices are of the "native informant" type. This is not exclusive to Muslim women. Many marginalized communities and groups suffer from the same phenomenon. I am not saying something new: in Canada, Blacks, Indigenous, and other people of colour are rarely accurately "represented" in their diversity and complexity.

When it comes to the question of hijab and Muslim women, personalities like Jamila Ben Habib in Quebec, Ayan Hirsi Ali in the US, and Zineb El Rhazoui in France have often occupied centre stage in the public debates, when the majority of Muslim women do not see themselves represented by them. The names and the personal experiences of these women, who have grown up in Muslim countries or societies, make them a de facto *porte-parole* for all Muslim women, despite sometimes by their own admission they have chosen not to believe or associate with Islam anymore. These women, favourites of the media, have claimed to be the voices of all Muslim women, thereby erasing all the differences among Muslim women—the diversity in their beliefs and practices and the traditions they come from. This is another flagrant demonstration of Islamophobia.

First, in the homogenizing project we have all to look the same; then, in order to introduce some controlled "diversity," we are divided into what author Mahmood Mamdani calls "Good Muslims" and "Bad Muslims." In the way these debates are framed, I would always be the Bad Muslim or the sore loser.

In Quebec, in the early 2000s, I was invited to some debates about the headscarf. At the beginning, I took them to be intellectual discussions, but I quickly realized that they were merely entertainment shows for the public. Not only were they light and superficial, but they also had intrinsic Islamophobic, misogynistic, and voyeuristic aspects to them. They reminded me of the time when bearded women were locked in cages and men and children came to laugh at them, or to women's wrestling matches with exclusive male audiences.

In these debates, the Good Muslim was usually a woman who was born a Muslim but was now a staunch secularist capable of hurling misleading stereotypes about Muslim women in the right accent. The more virulent her accusations were, the better the Muslim she was in the eyes of the audience, mainly white and ignorant. "Your hijab is the flagship of extremism" and "Hijab is the symbol of women's subservience," I was told once while sitting beside Julius Grey, a prominent Montreal human rights lawyer. We were invited to defend the liberty of religion and the values of acceptance. Our counterparts accused us of promoting fundamentalism and being apologists for oppression. No matter how misleading and fearmongering those arguments were, they would always win on a TV show.

The Good Muslim would show her allegiance to the values of modernity, of women's emancipation and freedom simply by her attractive looks and by the virulence of her statements. The fact that she was assumed to be Muslim, at least by her name or through her cultural background, made her a heroine, a brave freedom fighter revealing the truth about the headscarf and what it represents. Her personal attacks, under the rubric of "freedom of expression," were portrayed as examples of her courage. A Muslim woman wearing a headscarf, no matter how well constructed my arguments were and how important my truth was, I would lose the battle. With my hijab, I had implicitly vowed my allegiance to the values of backwardness, oppression, and subservience. The match was lost in advance.

I will always be judged through the symbolism of my headscarf and never according to my arguments or my explanations. That is why I stopped participating in those shows.

This is not a refusal for debate or expression. This a refusal in order to protect my mental health and not be an active participant in voyeurism matches where racialized women would be set against each other and where a personal and religious choice is rejected because it doesn't fit with one selective view of women's rights. These debates made me feel excluded rather than accepted. This is the essence of what a "wedge" issue in politics is. No matter whether a person is socially conservative or progressive, the picture of a woman in hijab becomes automatically associated with oppression and my choice will be dismissed as wrong.

Growing Up As a Muslim Woman in Tunisia

Tunisia is an official majority-Sunni Muslim country. Jews, Shia Muslims, Baha'is, and nonbelievers constitute less than 1 per cent of the population. Up to the independence of the country from the French in 1956, Islam was present in many aspects of the lives of Tunisians. Official Islam was represented by the person of the Bey, a king of the Husainid Dynasty (related to the Ottoman Dynasty) who reigned in Tunisia from 1705 until Mohamed al-Amin Bey was deposed by his prime minister, Habib Bourguiba, in 1957. There were religious institutions like the Zaytuna Mosque, one of the oldest educational and religious institutions in the Maghreb (North Africa), the Quranic Madrassa, called Kuttab, where the Quran was taught to children and young adults, charitable organizations with trust funds collected from zakat (voluntary charitable donations required by the Quran and collected by a central authority) and religious endowments called Habous. There were also popular forms of Islam present in cities, towns, and villages, in which popular saints were worshipped at their mausoleums, where food, candles, and incense were distributed, and ritual song recitals and Sufi dances took place during special occasions. The majority of urban women were secluded in the houses and when they stepped out, they wore the safsari, a length of white or beige silk fabric that covered the body. Some women also covered their faces with khama, another piece of fabric that hid the face and showed only the eyes.

Rural women's conditions were no better. They worked in farms and fields amidst poverty, disease, and ignorance. They usually wore a melia, a Berber outfit covering the entire body (two pieces of fabric, one attached at the shoulder level with special jewellery, and another at the waist with a type of a belt). Their hair was usually wrapped with a traditional scarf.

In cities, men wore a jebba, a traditional long and wide dress, and they usually covered their heads with either a chechia or a turban. In rural areas, men wore a quachabia, a wide long tunic made out of wool with an embedded hoodie on the top. Men had power over women in every aspect of life. Fathers, brothers, and husbands gave permission (or not) to the women to go outside for social gatherings, they held permission for them to go to school (even when education is a legal and religious right for women). They made decisions regarding inheritance (even when it is a religious right for women to inherit).

In general, the situation of women was bad. Their level of literacy was noticeably lower than men. They were doubly oppressed: by cultural patriarchy and by French colonialism, which ran the country and controlled all the bureaucratic and administrative institutions.

Recently I watched an old interview with a famous Tunisian singer, Naama, who had passed away a few years ago. She was born in 1934 under the French occupation and raised by her single mother in Tunis. To the question of why she didn't go to school, she replied candidly that the idea of sending her to a school run by nuns (most of the schools were run by the French) had been suggested to her mother by some friends but she refused. "My mother feared that by going to school, I would become a Christian. Instead, she sent me to a kuttab, a Quranic school, where I learned Arabic and memorized the Quran."[1] Ironically and counterintuitively, her education at the Quranic school, from learning the right pronunciations of Arabic to learning the different rhythms of the Quran recitations, helped her, by her own admission, in her singing career.

Many women didn't even have the opportunity to attend the Quranic school and were totally illiterate. They stayed home and raised families. But what made the situation of women worse was a certain literal and conservative interpretation of Islam, which rendered women subservient to men. Patriarchy was a strong tradition governing family relations, and Islam became the system that justified it. In the late nineteenth and early twentieth centuries, several secular thinkers and religious scholars, mostly men, asked for the reinterpretation of the Islamic texts regarding the status of women. In Egypt, considered the heart of the Arabo-Islamic world, religious voices like those of Jamaluddin Al-Afghani and Muhammad Abduh rose to call for a "fair" and "better" treatment of women. In Tunis, Tahar al-Haddad, a trade unionist, became one of these secular voices calling for reform. Al-Afghani and Abduh approached the need for reform through a liberating view of the religion itself, while al-Haddad and others took an exclusively rights approach inspired by liberal movements in Europe. Polygamy, female illiteracy, and the seclusion of women were some of the issues raised. New visions about the place of women in Islamic societies were put forward. Unfortunately these progressive calls were dismissed by religious scholars and the proposed reforms were shelved. The discussions remained restricted to intellectual and elite circles. No new readings of the religious texts succeeded in gaining acceptance.

Any attempt at reforming the status of women was associated with the colonizers, the French in the case of Tunisia or the British in Egypt, and thus frowned upon by the religious scholars and traditional and conservative leaders. With the division of Tunisian society into factions—urban and rural, conservative and liberal, traditionalist and reformist, nationalist and colonial-apologist, Arabophile and Francophile—the woman question became fractured and controversial.

What do we mean by the liberation of women? Who can bring it about? Should it come from within or outside of our society? How can our men fight the colonizer on one hand and accept the colonizer's ideas about "our women" on the other? Isn't the idea of women's liberation an attempt to divide us and corrupt our Islamic values? Is the religious class ready to "touch" the religious texts (with a view to reinterpret them)?

On one side was the belief that women's liberation (and certainly men's too) should begin with liberation from the rigid hold of religion on society. In its form and practice, religion was an obstacle to progress (including women's liberation), went the argument. It should be divorced from tradition, with which it had long become equated.

Moreover, the Sharia should be reinterpreted if it was to be applied. In this way the women would be liberated from seclusion and ignorance. In a nutshell, this view amounted to what we call secularism. Turkey, the former heart of the Ottoman Empire, which ruled many parts of the Islamic world (including Tunisia), became secular in the 1930s under the leadership of Mustafa Kemal. Some Tunisian politicians, including Bourguiba, looked at his new secular model with admiration.

On the other side, liberation from colonization, from French military and political domination, came first and foremost, along with the protection of Islamic values and the preservation of the Arabic language. In that regard, women were regarded as the guardians of Islamic values—whatever that meant—and any attempt to liberate them from religion was considered depravity and should be suppressed.

There were many other views in between these two poles. The general female population found itself entrapped and spoken for by one of those two corners, the liberal secularist and the conservative religious.

One thing was certain. In the postcolonial era, for both the secularists and the conservatives, (later called Islamists) patriarchy in itself was rarely questioned and the nation's progress became a top-down phenomenon. In 1956, Habib Bourguiba, the first president of the Tunisian republic following seventy-five years of French colonial rule, often considered the "Father of Independence," embraced a secular model for the "question of woman" and started a subtle policy of unveiling the women. This meant discouraging the face veil and the safsari long dress. The hijab, as we know it today—covering the hair—didn't exist.

Bourguiba didn't tackle the "question of woman" by itself. His reforms came in a secular package touching many aspects of Tunisian life. Zaytouna, the oldest religious institution, was banned, the habous, religious endowments created by the wealthy to support the poor and most vulnerable, were dissolved, and the regime took monopoly of the charitable sector. Religious practice was often called antimodernist. (In later years, Bourguiba would be accused by his political conservative opponents of attacking the Islamic character of Tunisia.)

To publicize and encourage the adoption of his policies, Bourguiba participated in "spontaneous" public ceremonies, where he removed the veils and the safsaris from the heads of women. Despite his claims of liberating women from "this odious rag," he was the perfect patriarchal figure. He claimed to "save" Tunisian Muslim women (and men) from ignorance. He twisted the arms of religious scholars, who were now appointed by him, to find religious justifications for banning polygyny (a man marrying several wives), repudiation, and divorce; to support the *Code du Statut Personel*, the reformed code that came to represent the feminist gains of Tunisian women; and to hail the nation's progress among the other countries.

To deny that this reform wasn't helpful and somehow daring would be untrue. My mother benefited from these feminist gains, as did I. Nevertheless, Tunisian feminism remained a state feminism, controlled by an elite that usually needed the approval of the president (the father figure) to move forward.

Many poor women benefited from accessible family planning, which helped them control their number of children and reduce poverty. Public education became available and mandatory for both boys and girls. The nascent textile industry offered thousands of jobs for poor young women in search of better economic prospects for their families. However, this feminism failed to become a grassroots movement capable of changing the mentalities of men and women. Patriarchal traditions remained entrenched despite the legal reforms.

In the 1970s and 1980s, the hijab as we know it today came into use. Safsari gradually disappeared from the urban landscape, as did jebba for men. These items of clothing became almost invisible in urban centres except when worn exclusively by older women and men. European attire was espoused by both sexes.

After the defeat of the Arab forces by Israel in 1967 and 1973, many Muslim countries saw the emergence of an "Islam renaissance." Islamic thinkers began to challenge the secularism that had come into Muslim countries after independence. The military defeat was interpreted and conveyed into the popular imagination as a failure of secularism, and Islamic revival was promised to be the solution. In universities around the Muslim world, several young men and women began to subscribe to this view. Tunisia wasn't an exception. The hijab now appeared in the streets of Muslim capitals where miniskirts and pants had ruled during the first years after independence. But now the hijab wasn't perceived as a sign of seclusion, as the safsari had been for their mothers and grandmothers, but rather it gave licence for going out to school or university, meeting men, or grabbing a place in the workforce, while still proudly maintaining an Islamic identity.

In the 1980s the long Bourguiba reign came to an end. Islamic groups became the main opposition to the regime, which now showed signs of weakness. The government focused on two religious symbols: hijabs in women and beards in men. A ministerial circular of 1981, numbered 108, targeted the public schools. It banned the hijab, calling it "a confessional dress." Three other ministerial circulars appeared. One introduced on August 12, 1987: it banned the hijab for officials at administrations and public establishments. On September 7, 1987, a circular banned the hijab in primary and secondary schools, and a third one introduced a few weeks later on September 21 banned the hijab in universities, including student residences.

On November 7, 1987, Bourguiba was deposed by his prime minister, Zine al-Abedine Ben Ali in a "medical coup." Bourguiba, deemed senile by a medical certificate, was declared incapable of running the country, in accordance with the Tunisian Constitution.

President Ben Ali continued the government's repression of its political opponents—the Islamists and what came to represent them, the hijab. In December 1991, yet another circular banned the hijab for those working in private institutions.

I grew up amidst these developments, torn between the dual oppressions of colonization and patriarchy on one hand and searching for freedom in my Islamic roots. I openly embraced my Muslim identity at the age of twenty and started wearing the hijab; at about the same time I learned about a disturbing aspect of my family history: the abuse and oppression of my maternal grandmother. My mother told me her story. She was illiterate, but an amazing woman who learned from her children, when she was in her forties, how to scribble her name. She raised seven children while her husband, my grandfather, was incapacitated by a neuro-degenerative disease that kept him at home and later caused his death.

My grandmother managed her household with intelligence and skill. Once she was offered a day job by the Red Cross to help at a community centre in her neighbourhood. When she mentioned this offer enthusiastically to her older brother, he slapped her in the face right in front of her young children. "We don't have women working outside the house," he told her angrily. My mother, who had witnessed the incident, related it to me in tears. I too wept as I recalled my grandmother's face. Her brother wasn't acting out of religious concern. He was not particularly religious but definitely oppressive. He was patriarchy's gatekeeper. He had probably thought: What will people think if my sister went to work outside the home? He might have felt hurt or useless in his role as a male brother who couldn't financially support his sister. Once again, religion packaged in traditions and customs offered a handy excuse for male domination. As if compassion, solidarity, and justice were not values of that same religion.

My decision to wear the hijab at the age of twenty would grow out of this somber past. How could I be myself without acknowledging the errors of those who came before me, acting in the belief that religion allowed them to abuse others, especially women and children?

This family history is the heavy burden I carry.

The Innocent Islamophobia

I first set foot in Canada in 1991. This was during the First Gulf War, and I had come to look for acceptance of who I was. In Tunisia, it was getting harder and harder for women wearing the hijab. For me Canada was the land of freedom, where my hijab wouldn't stand in the way for me to attend university and eventually work in the field I chose.

My first days, walking about and visiting people and places in Montreal, were uneventful. *Je passais inaperçue . . . ou presque.* On the streets there were not many women wearing the hijab and there were even fewer on the campus at the Université de Montréal where I was taking some courses in order to obtain "Canadian" credits for university qualification. But soon I realized that things were not as innocent they seemed at first.

I recall here a few incidents from my months and years in the city.

I was walking on a quiet street one day when a French Canadian woman stopped me. She looked nice and without any introduction asked me why I was wearing "that thing" on my head. I was fresh and naïve then and I felt important that people stopped me in the street to ask me questions. I was eager to prove to them that I had made a smart choice. I started explaining to the lady how hijab was my choice, how modesty was important for me, and how it was a relative concept.

"Didn't French Canadian women wear long skirts in the 40s and 50s? What was modest then is old-fashioned today and what is decent today was daring then. Everything is relative, isn't it? For me, hijab is like a compass. I don't need men's views or fashion trends to direct me . . . "

She was confused and annoyed by my preppy remark. She kept saying, "Yes, but . . . the veil is a sign of subjugation of women by men . . . " and I kept telling her that I was not wearing a veil and I was not oppressed by any man. I didn't have a husband who compelled me to wear a hijab, nor a father who had brainwashed me to do it. I was simply embracing my religion wholeheartedly.

She wasn't convinced at all, and I started losing patience with her. From seeming nice with me, the lady became authoritative and patronizing. I felt very uncomfortable. I wanted to leave.

"This is what you want to think of me. But I am not who you think I am," I told her. "Sorry, there is nothing else I can tell you."

Another time, I bumped into a professor I knew only slightly on the stairs of my business school, École des Hautes Études Commerciales, where I had enrolled now. It was 1993, a year after my arrival. He was going up and I coming down. He paused and asked me, "So do you wear this by choice or are you forced to do it?" Today, at my age, I would have replied, "That's not your business!" But I was naïve and still believed that I could change perceptions about my hijab. I didn't know yet how deep the prejudices ran in the culture I had come to.

His tone wasn't aggressive. He even sounded sympathetic. Maybe he thought he could save me from oppression. Maybe he was simply curious. In any case, I would have never dared asking a random man wearing shorts or a tie or a bow, or letting his hair grow long, or going bald a question about his appearance. Never would I stop or think of asking a woman in the street why she was dressed a certain way.

Later I understood that asking this question comes from a position of privilege that as a racialized Muslim woman I could never have. I also understood that replying to these questions was a sort of duty. I have to do it to show *patte blanche*. I have to be nice, understanding, and pleasant so I can convince the interrogating frontline, those who hold the truth (so they assume) and the privilege (which they have received from their history), and have accepted me into their country (which is not quite theirs), that I am harmless and grateful and, most of all, capable of making choices here. I have rarely changed the opinions of people about me, especially when it comes to hijab. It is beyond any rational discussion; it is about their personal beliefs and prejudices.

But beyond the personal story behind each hijab, there is the deeper and more complex story of the demonization of the hijab. I have learned over the years that being nice and smiling isn't going to change people's perception about the hijab. The misconceptions about hijab aren't going to be erased overnight by me patiently holding the door for another person, or with one random and hurried discussion on the street (or the stairs), or by a quick conversation on TV between a pro-hijab and an anti-hijab person.

When I tried my best to answer the French Canadian woman on the Montreal street about my reasons for wearing a hijab, I was on the spot and wanted to do my best. Later I asked myself over and over what could have pushed her to stop and question me. Was it simple curiosity? Was it a bad experience she had had while abroad on a trip in a majority Muslim country? Was it even a bad experience she had had while growing up in a religious school run by Catholic nuns? Or was it because of a book she had read or a movie she had watched, where the heroine was an oppressed Muslim woman?

When I joined the École des Hautes Études Commerciales that winter of 1993, I found the program coordinator very cold and her tone adversarial. I couldn't figure out what I had done wrong for her to treat me that way. I was new in the program and excited and viewed myself as polite and courteous. After seeing her interact warmly with another student, a French student from France, I took her attitude very personally, but I didn't want to make my life more miserable (being in grad school and still new in a country is hard enough). So I simply tried to forget about her.

In early summer that year, I went to her to ask about my final marks. That was the way to do it before the advent of the Internet. She was in her office and cold as usual, almost ignoring me. I moved closer to her desk while she was looking into my academic record. On a corner of her desk, there was a book. The cover had a picture of a woman in a headscarf. I moved even closer and stretched my neck in an attempt to decipher the title. It read: *Not Without My Daughter*. She finally got back to me with my marks. I thanked her and left, but my mind was still spinning from reading the title of that book. I knew it well. It is a story that became well known in the early 90s, about an American woman, Betty Mahmoody, who detailed her experiences of leaving the United States to go and live in Iran with her Iranian husband, and her subsequent escape from the country.

I couldn't stop linking the negative attitude that the program coordinator had shown towards me to her reading.

Not Without My Daughter portrays Islam and Muslim women in extremely negative terms. What started as a family dispute that happens every day around the world between a husband and a wife had given rise to a book full of prejudices and stereotypes about Muslim men, portraying them as violent and dishonest, Islam as misogynistic and cruel, and Muslim women as victims who are oppressed and subservient.

The book appeared in book clubs, on television programs, and in magazines, and the views of a whole generation of North Americans readers about Islam (and Iran as an Islamic country) were filled with the clichés found in the book and later in the movie that was based on it.

From a sad and true family story, where a husband abuses his rights, where patriarchal, legal, and political tools are hijacked by a male-dominated society to gain the custody of a daughter, and where an American wife and mother found herself powerless in a foreign country, the book became a bible of half-truths and problematic generalizations about Iranian men, about the relationships between men and women, about Islam and Islamic countries.

For many feminist groups in North America, Betty Mahmoody became an icon of feminism. For Homa Hoodfar, a Canadian Iranian anthropologist (who some years later was arrested and released by the Iranian regime) Mahmoody's book and the numerous talks she gave in America and Canada, became instrumental in intensifying the racism directed towards Muslim men in Canada. She even considered these talks as "fighting sexism (of Iranian men) with racism (of Canadian feminism)."[1]

Perhaps my program coordinator's reading only confirmed the pre-existing bias she had towards me as a Muslim woman wearing a hijab. I will never know the real reasons for her attitude. Nevertheless, I am comfortable to include her dislike of me and for the faith I represent in a bigger story, the one broadcast by media and perpetuated by popular culture.

In her book, *Do Muslim Women Need Saving?*, Lila Abu-Lughod dedicates a whole chapter to the portrayal of Muslim women in books. Betty Mahmoody's book is one of the books she describes. She calls such books "pulp fiction"—they not only shape the views of their readers, mostly women (through book clubs), but also mislead them into believing the myth that they know everything about Muslim women.

Perhaps for my program coordinator, despite my being a successful student in a highly competitive program, I was yet another oppressed Muslim woman, epitomized by my hijab. It didn't matter that she didn't know me personally—where and how I grew up, which books I read, what sports I played, was I poor or rich, which languages I spoke. All these questions that, in normal circumstances, help us forge friendships, or know and better understand and respect each other despite our differences, were apparently irrelevant. My image preceded me, aided with the "pulp fiction" narrative. I look like those Muslim female characters in a book they read or in a movie they watched. My father must have oppressed me, if not he then my brother, if not he then the boys in my neighbourhood, if not they, then some Muslim male, somewhere.

And even if I wasn't oppressed, or aware that I was being oppressed by Muslim men, my attire—a long-sleeved shirt, a long skirt, or a dress, with a headscarf, sent a message to the women out in the streets that I despised their pants, short skirts, and short-sleeved dresses. My mere physical presence was a threat to hard-won women's rights.

In the months and years that followed those early incidents, I had those arguments thrown at me over and over during question periods at conferences and on TV and radio shows, where I was constantly reminded of my oppression or the damage my appearance and religion were causing to women's rights. I stopped going to these shows. First of all, they have an entertainment component that dominates over any educational or informational intent that I think should be clear and unambiguous in every media program. The entertainment aspect consists of the excitement and the shallowness shown by the audience at seeing two women, usually "racialized," arguing. This happens when a media program invites two Muslim women to give polarized opinions about the headscarf or some other "Islamic" topic. I came to see those shows as women's fighting matches. One guest defends the hijab while the other is against it. This is an unfair fight, because usually the woman against hijab has lived longer in Quebec, if she's not born here, and is fluent in her ready-made crowd-pleasing views. I came out of these shows emotionally drained, asking myself why I had agreed to participate. I did so because I saw it as a duty. But I felt that the audience was more particularly interested in picking a "winner" rather than learning alternative views. The parallel with women's fighting matches was compelling. Finally, I stopped going to these media matches where I was already a loser before even standing in the ring. Now the tide is higher than it was thirty years ago. The myths are widespread, Hollywood and book marketers are efficient at perpetuating those myths, and the laws introduced by several Western democracies in the last couple of decades about the hijab, the niqab, and terrorism are all complicit in aggravating the persistent Islamophobia targeting Muslim women.

A Good Muslim or a Bad Progressive Woman?

People usually laugh or frown on hearing of "Islamic Feminism." How can we be both Muslims *and* Feminists? Isn't that a contradiction, a perfect oxymoron? Usually, according to mainstream understanding, a Muslim woman is a conservative, chauvinist, and misogynistic individual. On the other hand, a feminist is progressive, liberal, and a staunch believer of women's rights. These are of course simplistic and stereotypical descriptions. In my life, I have met Muslims who fit neither description and feminists who don't live up to their ideals.

Over the years, I have found that many of my actions and writings that would normally be described as progressive are questioned, let alone my attempts at feminism, or women's rights. My hijab puts doubt on my feminist credentials. What really matters for many of my critics are not my actions and words but how I look in my dress and hijab. I have also learned that for other critics, because of my views, I will never be a hundred per cent Muslim.

When I ran as a candidate in the Canadian federal election of 2004, three main controversies followed me, based on the following issues:

» Being a Muslim woman in politics.

» Shaking hands with men.

» My views on same-sex marriage.

According to a very rigorous and literalist interpretation of Islam, democracy isn't what Muslims should embrace in order to manage their political affairs but rather a concept called Shura.

Shura literally means "consultations." Prophet Muhammad, when faced with difficult questions and when a divine revelation hadn't arrived in time to guide him or remained silent, resorted to the opinions of his close friends and companions. He would ask for their advice, he listened to them, and then made his decision. This was a sort of band council. Diversity of opinions was sought and encouraged. However, if God finally revealed a different decision, it was always taken as the correct one. In some instances, the Prophet asked advice from the women, especially his youngest and smart wife, Aisha.

But for the older-generation and strictly rigorist Islamic interpreters, democracy is a foreign concept that should not be adopted by Muslims to decide on important communal affairs. Therefore, by embarking on a democratic journey and trying to gain votes to become a Member of Parliament, I was for some Muslims crossing a perilous boundary. My political involvement was seen as problematic at two levels. First, I was participating in the "un-Islamic" practice of "democracy," and second, I was taking on a man's role and letting down my duties as a mother and wife. I even received an email from a Muslim woman I didn't know, saying, "Take care of your children and husband, dear sister, this is what you should really do."

Perhaps, this "sister" meant well for me. According to her, apparently, my involvement in the political campaign represented a threat to a strictly preassigned, predefined role for a Muslim woman. On the same campaign trail, I was hugely criticized by some Muslims (men and women) because I shook hands with men, Muslims and non-Muslims.

The late Jack Layton, the former leader of the New Democratic Party of Canada (NDP), during our first meeting, looking at me in the eyes, said, "Monia, how do you want me to greet you?" He knew, or somebody from his staff must have told him about the taboo aspect of shaking hands with Muslim women. This was the first time someone had asked me about my own feelings towards an act that is supposed to be a consensual gesture in Western society. I have always been put on the defensive: If I don't shake hands, I am a conservative or a fundamentalist. If I shake hands, I am a liberal, a feminist, and too much integrated into Western culture, a sell-out to my Muslim community.

But what about me? How do I feel?

I grew up where shaking hands was a practice reserved mainly among men, but it could occur in formal and official meetings between men and women. It was very rare among women themselves. Between family members, we kissed each other on the cheeks. I remember myself as a young girl and even later as a teenager, greeting my uncles, my male relatives (older or younger than me), and my father's friends with kisses on both cheeks. Usually, older women didn't kiss unrelated males, and shaking hands would be more appropriate in formal circumstances. Women would kiss each other on the cheeks, even if they met for the first time. Men would also kiss each other on both cheeks if they were friends and close relatives. In high school and later at university, like everybody else I would greet my male friends with a kiss on both cheeks.

When I decided to wear the hijab, I stopped all these traditional and cultural practices. I wanted a clear physical boundary between me and unrelated males. I didn't want to touch or be touched by strangers, even with an innocent handshake. By wearing a hijab, I implicitly told all males that they couldn't touch me. Of course, that didn't go down well. I became the "fundamentalist," the "Muslim brotherhood sympathizer," the "radical"—even among my family and my friends.

Today, thinking about my attitude then, I find it a bit naïve and somewhat childish. I wanted to change the world and apply my own rules. But it was probably an inevitable step in building my whole identity. I was looking for solid reference points and hand-shaking seemed to me at that time a crucial delimiter.

Living in Canada made me reassess my values.

I started shaking hands when required because that made my life easier; I didn't want each time to provide a long explanation about my personal and religious beliefs. I adopted the practice because it is part of the accepted social etiquette of greeting each other in Canada. It is a matter of perceived politeness. But that doesn't make shaking hands a universal value. In fact, for some autistic people physical touching is a source of deep discomfort.

Many times, I heard from non-Muslim men how offended they were when Muslim women refused to shake their hands. They said this after I had shaken their hands, as though this made me their ally. I wish I had had the audacity to reply to those men, "Have you ever thought how these women would feel if they had to shake your hands?"

Thus, by publicly shaking hands with men, I immediately became labelled by some Muslims as a liberal, meaning a "loose" Muslim woman.

My decision to run for federal politics was encountered in some media with pure cynicism. The *Ottawa Citizen* ran an editorial where they qualified me as a "sacrificial lamb" of the NDP and said further that my husband's pending public inquiry at that time would jeopardize my future political career in case my husband was indicted or not cleared from terrorism association. The implication was that I had no standing without my husband, hence, bringing into the debate another patriarchal and patronizing attitude, usually associated with Islam but this time used against me by my supposed "liberators."

In 2004 the same-sex marriage issue was brought up frequently during the election campaign. The former finance minister, Paul Martin, who was running as head of the liberal party promised to implement it, if elected. The late Jack Layton, who had been elected as the leader of the NDP and who was running for his first parliamentary seat, also made it clear that all the NDP candidates should follow the party line on this issue.

I became a problem. I am a practicing Muslim woman, and my position was constantly challenged. From the beginning, I made my position clear: as a deeply religious person I couldn't vote for same-sex marriage. However, as a human rights activist, I couldn't prevent two people from entering into a marriage relationship, and thus if elected I promised that I wouldn't vote against it. I would abstain in order to not contradict my own religious beliefs but without hurting other people's choices.

I was confident and content with my decision and I shared it with the party. Jack Layton and Alexa McDonough, a former leader of the NDP, who recruited me into the party, respected my position. Perhaps they thought that I would never win and so would not be an embarrassment for the party. In any case, both of them were fine with my position.

However, inside the party and with some activists the tension was palpable. I read the emails sent to the party leadership regarding my candidacy. I was considered homophobic. My headscarf was considered disrespectful to centuries of women's struggles and a sign of violence and persecution of women in Muslim countries. There were calls for my removal from the party. I wasn't a true New Democrat. And so on.

Same-sex marriage became a wedge issue. I was judged according to that prism. It didn't matter that I was calling for more funding for social housing. It didn't matter that I was a voice for public health care. It didn't matter that I was aligned with all the calls for a national childcare system. It didn't matter that I clearly said that I wouldn't vote against the bill because I believe in human rights. The fact that I would abstain from voting for the same-sex marriage bill if elected, made me an imposter to some social justice activists.

For some Muslims, on the other hand, I wasn't being true to my religious convictions. I lacked the courage to stand up against those who were violating the definition of marriage that considered it as a union between a man and a woman. I was a hypocrite. Another Muslim woman candidate in a headscarf, who was running during the same campaign in British Columbia, promised to vote for the same-sex marriage bill. We spoke with each other with sympathy and understanding. She told me that her father had been viciously criticized in his mosque by people who thought he didn't know how to raise his daughter properly.

Clearly, we Muslim women will always fail to live up to the standards of one group or the other. Once, while distributing leaflets near the Billing Bridge station in Ottawa, about the importance of funding for public transportation, an anti-abortion activist approached me. He saw me in my hijab as a natural ally. He told me I should vote against abortion if elected. He didn't know that abortion was legalized in Tunisia in 1965, way before Canada and other European countries, and that I grew up with women who accessed abortion through private and public clinics. That didn't make abortion an easy and noncontroversial topic in Tunisia, a Muslim country, but it never had as in Canada the heavy historical and violent history directed towards women who advocated abortion rights. Once again, I was judged through the narrow and misleading lens coloured by my hijab.

For some I wasn't a true progressive, for others I wasn't a good Muslim. I found myself thrown out from any group I tried to join in order to establish an identity for myself, and this brought me to that precarity of what I once called being a bastard. Never belonging fully to where you think you should be. That precarity in status or the bastard qualification returned years later when a friend encouraged me to apply for a job in the field of community diversity. I never got the job. I was not even invited for an interview, because some members on the hiring committee were not comfortable with my decision to abstain from voting for "same-sex marriage" in 2004.

More recently, I was heading a literary competition and a candidate commented publicly on the organization's Instagram account that he hoped my 2004 position on same-sex marriage would not hurt his chances as a gay candidate. This statement was wounding. Abstaining from a vote on same-sex marriage is not the same as voting against it; it is not homophobic and not out of hatred, which "phobia" signifies. It is a position that respects my religious beliefs as well as other people's choices. Assuming that my hijab would automatically discriminate against other people's beliefs or sexual orientations is really disturbing. Unfortunately, we live in an increasingly polarized world, where there is no room for nuance. You are either "this" or "that." And of course, I find myself always to be "that."

Diversity isn't always synonymous with acceptance and understanding. If you are accepted despite your race, you could be rejected for your religious beliefs. And vice versa. I understand why some people disagree with my position regarding same-sex marriage, but I don't think I should be censured or removed. A similar situation could arise regarding my headscarf. I don't expect people to love my choice, but the least they can do is to respect me and to listen to my story.

After I published my first memoir, while I was on my book tour, I was invited by my friend Michael Byers and his wife Katharine at their place in Vancouver for a small reception. One of their friends came to me and expressed his appreciation for my work to clear my husband's name. With tears in his eyes, he told me, "As a gay man, I understand the oppression you went through, because it happened to us too . . . We had to go to the courts for our rights." I was shaken by his words of solidarity. This is how we should see ourselves, I thought, working with each other in our fights, and move towards an inclusive society. My religious beliefs should be respected and protected as much as the rights of this man who courageously brought both our fights to the same level.

Hijab and Employment

In 2000 I applied for an assistant professorship in finance at the University of Ottawa, for which I was invited for an interview. Among those conducting the interview was a PhD student from a Montreal university. We had taken some mandatory courses together, but he hadn't defended his thesis yet, and here he was on the hiring committee. I was told by another member of the committee that my candidacy was excellent: a PhD in finance from a prestigious university, fluently bilingual and living in Ottawa. Everyone gave me the impression that I was the ideal candidate. Instead, a short while later I received a curt reply to tell me that my position wouldn't be filled due to budget cuts. But deep inside me, I knew that my headscarf had been a problem. Years later, I was told very quietly by a long-time professor that my look didn't please everyone, and that in order to find a job, I had to be more discreet and less obvious in my clothing choices, meaning my hijab.

This only confirmed my gut feeling, or as my mother would put it, what my heart told me. The same scenario had occurred not long before with my alma mater, École des Hautes Études Commerciales de Montréal. One day, I learned from some of my PhD colleagues that my former master's degree supervisor at the École des Hautes Études Commerciales of Montreal was trying to reach me in my McGill office by phone. I phoned him back. He sounded happy and told me, "We are looking for a finance professor and I think your candidacy would be excellent."

It was my dream. Working as a finance professor in a business school where I studied once. Most of the professors there knew me. I was confident that they had excellent opinions of me. I had worked as a research and teaching assistant for some, including my own supervisor. One of the new professors was a former PhD from McGill, supervised by the same professor, and he had been on my thesis defence committee. In short, I was in friendly territory.

At that time, my husband was working with Matlab, a software engineering company in Boston, Massachusetts. I was staying in Ottawa with our four-year old daughter, finishing my thesis. My husband moved back and forth between the two cities. The enthusiasm shown by my master's supervisor, my acquaintance with most of the faculty members, the trust and friendship they had showed during the two years I was with them, and my comfort at teaching finance in French— all this made me believe that I would be hired. I started planning for my new life in Montreal.

The only issue was my husband's job. How could he leave a very good job in the US and come to live in Montreal? I spoke with my husband, and we agreed that if he could get some help finding a job in Montreal, we would move there. My professor told me that he knew some venture capitalists who could help my husband start his own business. What more could I dream of? A job at my previous business school, a husband working in the same city, and a life in Montreal, the city I love and never wanted to leave ever since I first landed in Canada.

But my excitement came to an end abruptly after I was invited for an interview. Many professors on the hiring committees knew me. I spoke about my empirical model, my results, and my findings. I was taken for lunch with three professors including my supervisor, who had approached me. Then came the wait for the committee decision. I waited and waited for an email or a letter. Silence.

Finally, a letter came from my master's supervisor, informing me that they had received "thousands of applications" and that the decision was hard and that my candidacy was declined.

I was crushed.

I would never have applied for that position if my supervisor hadn't encouraged me.

Was this all a game to create the impression that the university was into diversity? Was I the "diverse" candidate? Am I that incompetent that I failed to convince the committee that I deserved to be hired? Perhaps the excitement shown by my professor had given me a false signal. But when you are the chair of the hiring committee, I assume you have enough experience not to give so many false signals to your preferred candidate without speaking to your colleagues and without being confident in your choice.

Worse, the letter had spoken of "thousands of applications." This was such an extreme exaggeration that I didn't know whether to cry or laugh. I did both.

In Quebec, there are a very small number of universities that give PhD degrees in finance. At McGill, the year I started my program, we were four PhD students. One of them never finished. Another went back home after he defended his thesis. I had defended successfully and gone to work in the private sector, and the fourth one was still working on her thesis. If we included those who graduate with a doctorate every year in economics, applied mathematics, and finance from Quebec, we barely reach a dozen. If we add those applying from France or the US, we might reach a couple of hundred at most.

So, thousands of applications? It was absurd. I was left with two real reasons for my rejection:

A candidate was better than me.

My hijab.

Both reasons were deeply hurtful, more so the second one. I felt that my hijab had created a barrier for my career. Academic decisions can be very subjective, despite the myth of rationality. Anyone familiar with academic departments would be familiar with the constant squabbles, infighting, and bargaining going on. The end result of all that was that I began doubting myself. It took me many years to forget this incident.

In 2007, I was hired as an assistant professor of finance at the Thompson Rivers University, a former community college turned into a university in Kamloops, British Columbia.

It was my dream came true, albeit somewhat muted.

I had to leave Ottawa and go far away from my friends and my family for this dream job. With a PhD in finance, one can normally find work in the high finance sector—private investment companies and banks—and in academia. But only if you are a white man. It was only a few years ago when white women started to slowly make their way up there. For a person of colour, especially one wearing a headscarf, the picture is bleak.

My experience in academia is not an isolated or exceptional story. In their book *The Equity Myth: Racialization and Indigeneity at Canadian Universities*, the authors debunk the myth that was built over decades about the diversity of our Canadian universities, and speak about the unfulfilled promise for racialized and indigenous academics despite some initiatives to address the problems. In 2018, the Canadian Association of University Teachers (CAUT) released a report on the state of diversity and equity among Canada's postsecondary education institutions. The report found that lack of diversity is an ongoing problem. Indeed, the work force seems to be nowhere near as diverse as the student body at these institutions, which are busy recruiting in Canada and overseas to increase their budgets.

Even more surprising is a 2016 Canadian study that found that first- and second-generation children of immigrants had a higher presence in postsecondary institutions than others (86.6 and 83.0 per cent respectively vs 71.2 per cent). Clearly, it isn't so much the lack of qualified Indigenous and People of Colour candidates as the obstacles of racial and other discrimination they face in getting hired at postsecondary institutions.

When I was hired at the Thompson Rivers University Business School, I received some hate mail directly targeting my hijab. One anonymous letter called it a "rag." It was sent to my faculty address, and I was very shaken by it. I showed it to the administration. They were sympathetic but that didn't go beyond words.

At the end of that school year, my husband and I took the decision to come back to live in Ottawa. It was a hard decision for me. Despite all the challenges I faced, I wanted to keep my academic job. I had worked so hard to get it. But my aging in-laws were in Montreal, and they needed my husband's support. My children were among the few Muslim children in their schools in Kamloops and I found myself overwhelmed trying to teach them Arabic on Sunday. My week was divided as follows: four days of teaching at the University, one day of administrative duties, and two days teaching my own kids, caring for the house, and preparing for my next classes. I lacked the support of a community and Ottawa represented all that I missed. Therefore, I resigned. I don't know if that qualifies as a perfect example of "emotional labour" exhaustion, but I am convinced that I sacrificed my career for the well-being of my family. Many women did that and still do. My professional career isn't merely a question of my competence and skills, it is related to my visibility and the perception people have of me, my family situation, my financial income, my children's educational success, my cultural integration, and other factors. As a society we have to admit that for years we pretended that race, gender, religion, and sexual orientation weren't factors of discrimination. We claimed we were the champions of multiculturalism. The reality on the ground was different. I am happy to see recently that many voices from minority communities are demanding real changes: a real representation in academia, the inclusion of serious antiracism conversations in universities without the fear of censorship, etc. These issues are difficult but important. They require us to question the foundations of our society, its history of racism and colonialism.

We are at a crossroads. Putting our heads in the sand isn't an option. Looking away isn't an option. Working together to bring about positive changes is the only viable option.

Hijab and Public Transit

In the summer of 2019, I was on a bus heading from Gatineau to Ottawa. I was taking that route for the first time and wasn't familiar with the stops on the way. When I thought my stop was next, I rang the bell, signalling my intention to get off. It turned out that I was wrong, we were still far from my stop, and so I didn't get off. A white, middle-aged man standing beside me asked, "Why didn't you get off?" Taking his question at face value, I replied, "I made a mistake." To my surprise, he was quick to fire back: "Next time, don't do it!"

I was shocked. The bus driver hadn't said a word, and yet here was this random man who felt entitled to rudely reprimand me. "Don't talk to me that way," I replied, fuming. "Shut up!" he retorted angrily. "You shut up," I replied back. "I am going to report you to the bus driver."

A white woman then stood up, came over, standing between me and the man, and inquired, "Is there anything I can do to help?" The whole dynamic of the situation changed. Until then, I was the isolated Muslim woman facing a white male bully, and now this white woman had decided to break the "domination" relationship and turn it into an alliance. In a matter of seconds, a Black woman joined the circle, saying in a light tone, "What is the problem here? I always make mistakes when requesting bus stops." A racialized man, who had been quietly watching, was emboldened to say, "Why are you behaving this way?" The offender, isolated, retreated.

No longer on the offensive, he said he was "just wondering." "No,"

I corrected him, "You were simply mean." He didn't say a word. I was still shaken, but because of the solidarity around me, I decided to go to the bus driver and tell him about what had just happened. He was very cooperative. "If you want me to report him, I can do it immediately; I can even kick him off the bus." I was not on a power trip. I was just trying to go home. I told him that this time I would let it go, and soon after I got off at my stop. The white and Black ladies who had stood by me both got off at the same stop; I thanked them for their support, and each of us went on her way.

This incident looks trivial on the surface, but it disturbed me, physically and morally. I thought I was much stronger than that, but obviously I was not. I thought that my words should come more easily to my rescue, but they had come out trembling and slow. I speak three languages. It is known that in tense and emotional circumstances, when a person is at risk or in a situation of fear, she finds it easier to communicate in her mother tongue. But not only did I reply to this man in English but also in a manner that accurately reflected my emotions. I was so overwhelmed when I reached home that I felt I needed to cry.

Crying helped ease the great anger raging inside me, but it also brought me to acknowledge my humanity—the simple humanity I constantly have to prove exists under my hijab. Since the attacks of 9/11, I've felt insecure on the street. As a woman wearing a hijab, I became an easy target for glares, rude behaviour, bigotry at all levels, and Islamophobic comments. I am not claiming that I am constantly a victim. Nevertheless, my fears are always in the back of my mind and unconsciously or consciously they shape my actions and my attitudes, my words and my silences. The hypervigilant state that I always find myself in drains me emotionally, and nothing can calm me down until I am at home.

Despite who I think I am or how I describe myself, my appearance speaks more quickly than I can in public spaces. The decade-long hammering by the media regarding the question of "reasonable accommodation" in Quebec; the attempt later to ban "religious symbols" specifically targeting women in hijab by Quebec premier Pauline Marois in the 2013 provincial election; and, following that, the campaign against the niqab carried out enthusiastically by former Canadian prime minister Stephen Harper in 2015, created a state of nervous vigilance in many Canadian Muslims.

These tactics of identity politics are not merely political experiments that magically disappear once an election is over or after a politician is defeated. They are not merely words that fade away with time; they have a long-lasting impact on people, and they can lead inevitably to reactions.

The dehumanization that Muslim women are subject to—either through classic Orientalist depictions in paintings like *Women of Algiers in Their Apartment* by Eugène Delacroix or through stereotypes like the cute Jasmine character in the Hollywood film *Aladdin*—becomes ingrained in people's imaginations. The common, simplistic and wrong perception that the hijab is a symbol of oppression is still alive and thriving, even though many books have been written by Muslim women to declare otherwise.

I don't know what exactly pushed that man on the bus to confront me the way he did. Was it just the fact that I was a woman? Or that I was wearing a headscarf, which invested him with the mission of teaching me a lesson? Was it resentment against alien immigrants? One can never know for certain. However, as someone who lived through that experience, looked into his eyes, saw his expression, and heard his tone, I have little doubt that he wouldn't have spoken to me the way he did if I wasn't a woman wearing a headscarf.

A report in 2018 declared, "One in four Muslim women wearing a headscarf in New York City has been pushed on a subway platform." So I have every cause to feel insecure.

Moya Bailey, a queer Black feminist, has coined the term "misogynoir" to describe misogyny towards Black women, where race and gender both play a role in bias. "Misogynijab" would perhaps be the term to use in those cases where misogyny and hijab both contribute to the hatred of women.

Populist politicians, with their simplistic and dangerous rhetoric, contribute to the negative behaviour—such as attacks on minorities—in their supporters. The words of people like Donald Trump and Stephen Harper are not simple talk and controversial tweets. Their impact falls upon vulnerable people in the streets, on public transit, and inside detention centres.

I have never considered myself oppressed. In fact, I think I am privileged. I came to Canada to pursue graduate studies. I have a family. I have a house and I drive a car. If I hadn't taken the bus that day, the incident I have related above wouldn't have happened, and I would have thought that the world is still a wonderful place and Canada the most tolerant country. But obviously, it is not.

If I had been some refugee or a hijab-wearing woman who doesn't speak much English, what would have been the outcome on that bus? What if the two women who offered support had not been there? What if everyone else behaved like bystanders, unconcerned by what was happening? What if the bus driver had been uncooperative, or worse, indifferent? Most likely, the white man would have been more abusive.

In May 2016, the driver of an OC Transpo bus, along with some passengers, intervened when a man hurled Islamophobic taunts at a Muslim woman wearing a niqab, the full-face cover. Alain Charette, the driver, pulled the bus over and told the man that he had called the authorities. The man left the bus, and the Muslim woman, Hailey DeJong, thanked the driver. Alain Charette became a hero for the Muslim community. After he passed away, he was fondly remembered by Ihsaan Ghardee, executive director of the National Council of Canadian Muslims as "very humble and did not want to be called a hero, although that is what he was to many in the Muslim community." His daughter, Chloé Charette said that her father "was a strong believer in equality for everyone."[1]

The two women in my own experience, and the driver who stood up against the abusive man, behaved "normally," but for me they were also heroes. Keeping quiet when someone is being insulted or bullied is wrong and cowardly.

Hijab and the Media

In his iconic book, *Orientalism*, Edward Said, an Arab Christian from Palestine, detailed the stereotypes of the violent Arab man and the submissive Muslim woman that have been perpetuated by Hollywood. He wrote "In newsreels or news-photos, the Arab is always shown in large numbers. No individuality, no personal characteristics or experiences. Most of the pictures represent mass rage and misery, or irrational (hence hopelessly eccentric) gestures. Lurking behind all of these images is the menace of jihad. Consequence: a fear that the Muslims (or Arabs) will take over the world."

In an interview for Media Education Foundation, where he discusses his book, he elaborates, "It's the situation in the popular media . . . that basically Muslims are really two things . . . they are villains and fanatics."[1]

In the previous pages, I have already written about recent books and movies that distort and stereotype Islam and Muslim women. They freeze Muslim women into clichés and stereotypes, from which it is almost impossible to break free.

In an interview on Muslim representation in the media, H A Hellyer, a fellow at the University of Cambridge in the UK, declared:

> If we compare how Muslims are portrayed in English-language entertainment media—British, American, Australian and New Zealand television—the situation has

certainly improved over the past decade. That is not necessarily as positive as one might assume, however, because we would have been starting from a pretty low bar. The impact of the internet and social media over the past decade has meant that media companies and news outlets come under a lot more pressure from the public to address issues in different ways. I'm not saying things have become perfect—they haven't. But there's definitely been progress.[2]

Recently there have been some positive portrayals of Muslims in the entertainment media.

In 2007, Zarqa Nawaz, a Canadian author and producer for film and television, created the CBC comedy series *Little Mosque on the Prairie*, the world's first sitcom about a Muslim community living in the West. It was a revolutionary moment for Canadian Muslims in particular but also for others. Muslims who were for years portrayed as violent and angry, became the subjects of humour and funny quid pro quo. Women in hijab were shown on national TV as educated and capable of making their own decisions. That was the first Canadian production to bring Muslim characters out of the stereotypical mould. Despite some criticism, *Little Mosque* remains a model of how television and films can become tools for combatting ignorance, racism, and Islamophobia.

In the UK, in 2021 Channel 4 brought out a new comedy *We Are Lady Parts* written by Nida Manzoor that focuses on the lives of the all-female members of a Muslim punk band from east London. The diversity of the female Muslim characters in the series, in their race, sexual orientation, and approach towards their faith, was an excellent deconstruction of the homogenous stereotype that for decades had painted Muslim women with the same brush of oppression, terrorism and submission.

Despite such positive examples, Islamophobia remains present in our media. Two recent incidents highlight the essence of Islamophobia. Both occurred during the same week in January 2021.

The first concerned the appointment of Omar Alghabra, a long-time

Liberal MP born in Saudi Arabia to Syrian parents, as Minister of Transportation in the Trudeau government. The second was the hiring of Ginella Massa, the first Black Muslim woman journalist wearing hijab, as host of *Canada Tonight*, a nightly program on the national CBC News Network.

Beyond the excitement that those two distinct events generated for a lot of people, and the important symbolism of these appointments in terms of diversity and inclusion (I won't comment on the political or public-relations motives behind these appointments.), in Quebec there was a huge outcry from politicians, journalists, and other commentators.

The two appointees were both Canadians living in Toronto and English speakers. It was as if *les deux solitudes* had become a more acute symptom, the rift between French and English Canada had grown deeper. Now it wasn't only language and culture that caused the gap between the two but also the idea and practice of diversity.

Omar Alghabra was hinted by the leader of the Bloc Québécois to belong to "Political Islam" and by extension to the Muslim Brotherhood. According to its leader, Yves-François Blanchet, "creeping sharia" was invading "us."[3] Despite being criticized for his false accusations, Blanchet kept raising the spectre of Hamas, a Palestinian organization classified as terrorist by the Canadian government, which decision was opposed by Alghabra when he was the executive director of the Canadian Arab Federation (CAF).

A legal challenge of that classification doesn't make someone a terrorist or a terrorist sympathizer. It is common for some groups to be added to the list and others to be removed. The Afghan Mujahideen, for example, were described as freedom fighters by the United States in the 1980s and welcomed to the White House as heroes by President Ronald Reagan later; in the aftermath of the September 11, 2001 attacks, they became "terrorists" once more and Afghanistan was invaded in 2002 by the Americans. In a democracy, a government's decisions can always be challenged. Nelson Mandela was for decades listed as a terrorist, later he was a Nobel Peace Prize recipient and an international icon for civil rights movements.

Blanchet's insinuations were a clear tactic of using "guilt by association." An Arab Muslim man, who represented an advocacy organization (CAF) that provided services to the Arab diaspora, Muslims and non-Muslims alike, challenged a political decision and was immediately associated with terrorism. The stereotype of the terrorist Arab Muslim is irresistible. It is evoked with no shame or fear of consequences.

This is a perfect example of Islamophobia.

What is ironic and unfortunate is that the defence against those insinuations by some journalists was also problematic. "The Bloc's sneaky slur against a mild-mannered Muslim MP" was the title of an article written by Campbell Clark in the *Globe and Mail*. A "mild-mannered Muslim MP"! It is as if a Muslim man is expected to be violent normally.

In 2007, John McCain, a former American presidential nominee, came to the rescue of President Obama, who was attacked for being a "secret Muslim," a smear spread by Donald Trump and his followers. McCain described Obama in the following terms:

"He's a decent family man [and] citizen that I just happen to have disagreements with on fundamental issues, and that's what the campaign's all about. He's not [an Arab]."[4]

A perfect example of gendered Islamophobia is what happened to Ginella Massa, a Canadian Latina Muslim woman. After her first appearance on air on CBC TV, a well-known and controversial columnist, Richard Martineau, wrote a column in *Journal de Montreal*, asking the sarcastic question, "So when will we see a TV anchor on air wearing the cross?"

The message here was that Muslims were allowed (by a national institution, the CBC) to wear their religious symbols on air whereas Catholics could not do the same. There was also the insinuation in that column that a Muslim woman in hijab as CBC anchor was just the tip of the iceberg. The rest of the iceberg was all the other Muslims waiting and ready to take over other Canadian institutions and impose sharia on Canadians. This is of course the well-known myth of the Trojan horse brought here to scare people about Muslims and Islam. The idea of Muslims taking over European civilization became so widespread in the popular imagination and mainstream culture that Michel

Houellebecq, a well-known French novelist, made it the subject of his book, *Submission*.

Josée Legault, the Quebec political commentator, in a column in *Le Journal de Montréal*, reminded readers about the importance of skills before appearance. The false parallel between the Catholic cross and the hijab stirs fears about the possible takeover of Quebecois society by Islam and Muslims and the disappearance of the province's French Catholic character. But the ban of religious symbols at civic institutions was not imposed by Muslims. It was a reaction to the centuries-long domination of Quebec society by the Catholic church, before the *Révolution tranquille* of the 1960s removed it.

These are clear examples of the distortion of Islam and the Muslim presence in Canada by media commentators and politicians. But they could have happened in any province or territory in Canada. The political and cultural tensions between the French and Anglo Canadian models of integration might give the impression that Quebec is more Islamophobic than the rest of Canada. This is not true. Islamophobia exists everywhere, even in Muslim countries. It is wrong to be distracted by this false premise: which province or what cultural model is more Islamophobic than others.

Three terrible Islamophobic acts of violence by young Canadian white males illustrate this point.

> » The Quebec City Mosque attack in 2017 that killed six men and injured nineteen others.

> » The fatal stabbing of Mohamed-Aslim Zafis, a volunteer caretaker at the International Muslim Organization (IMO) Mosque in Rexdale, west of Toronto, Ontario, in 2020.

> » The killing of four members of a Muslim family in London, Ontario in 2021.

Later in this book, I will detail Islamophobic attacks on Muslim women in Canada. It is clear that Islamophobia isn't restricted to a Canadian province, or a certain language or culture or people. It happens wherever hate is left unchallenged to fester and perpetuate.

Hijab and Politics

When I dreamed of coming to Canada, I never thought for a single minute that there might come a day when a provincial law in Quebec would be passed to ban religious symbols, including the hijab I was wearing. At the time Canada had been described to me as a place of freedom. Constantly judged in Tunisia for my hijab, I saw Canada as a land of freedom, where I could study, work, and do whatever I wanted without being singled out, harassed, or judged for my religious attire. I was twenty-one years old and didn't know much about the nation's past or the conditions of Black and Indigenous people.

A few years after I landed in Montréal, I started hearing controversies about the hijab. They were sporadic. The case of a young girl kicked out of her private school because of her hijab; a white journalist who for one week wore the hijab and then wrote about her experiment in negative and offending terms to women in hijab. Until the 2000s, the "hijab question" was never explicitly embraced by any political party; it was a "lone wolf" topic, it existed but didn't make it into the news very frequently. The only and divisive question was independence. Soon, however, the hijab topic took over and worked itself up to a crescendo, with politicians and media commentators jumping in with opinions and fears.

During every provincial election, the Quebec independence question came as a final threat launched by the "federalist" Parti Libéral du Québec (PLQ) to dissuade the last batch of hesitant voters from siding with the sovereigntist Parti Québécois (PQ). This polarization worked relatively well, at least to a certain extent, for the PLQ. But after the loss of the 1995 referendum by the Quebec sovereigntists, the independence movement has been losing ground, especially among younger voters; even the baby boomers, usually supporters of the idea, have been showing signs of weariness.

Over the years, the focus in Quebec politics has shifted from independence to identity. It was Mario Dumont, forefather of today's Coalition Avenir Québec (CAQ), (which is now governing in Quebec), who was instrumental in bringing the inflated "reasonable accommodation" debate into Quebec's political affairs.

For a while, political fearmongering stopped targeting federalist Anglos, who were seen as threats to French culture with their imperialistic language, songs, movies, and powerful economic institutions. Instead, it was directed—skilfully, with media complicity—at a new threat: immigrants and more particularly, Muslim and Arab immigrants.

During the 1990s and early 2000s, many French-speaking North Africans, especially Algerians, started immigrating to Montreal. At the time Algeria was going through a dark and violent chapter: ruthless military regime fighting with different Islamist groups. And so from being exotic, the hijab became visible in the streets, schools, public administration, and public transportation of Montreal. In response, parroting what politicians had already done in France during their campaigns, introducing the identity debate, the immigration question, and French nationalism, Quebec politicians gradually discovered they too could make political gains with the same issues. The "reasonable accommodations" era was born.

Story after story appeared in the media demonstrating the apparent absurdity of accommodation. A Hassidic Jewish group complained about scantily clad women at a nearby gym being visible to their students through the glass walls; the gym replaced the walls with frosted glass. A group of Muslim families went to a sugar bush demanding no-lard dishes. A young Sikh man from Montreal insisted on wearing his kirpan (a ritual dagger) in school. A teenage Muslim girl wanted to wear a hijab during her soccer match.

Such stories were amplified and exaggerated by the media to look like dangerous absurdities, and the panic that was consequently instilled

69

in the minds of French Canadians brought back memories of British colonialism. The difference this time was that "immigration" and "barbaric cultural practices" were the villains threatening to take over their culture. Hijab, halal food, kirpan, and kippa became wedge issues. The bodies, cultures, and religious practices of immigrants and minorities became the playgrounds of the politicians and the media.

In the 2007 Quebec election, the Action Démocratique du Québec (ADQ), headed by Mario Dumont, a small and marginal political party at the time, won forty-one seats in the National Assembly and against all odds became the official opposition, sending the Parti Québécois into third position. That victory marked the beginning of a new era: the replacement of the independence question by identity politics.

Under a lot of political pressure and to temporarily calm down tensions and put the controversial topic out of his political agenda, Jean Charest, premier of Quebec, launched the Taylor-Bouchard Commission to look at the questions raised by "reasonable accommodation" and propose solutions.

For me, this was the worst outcome possible. Instead of finding solutions to combat racism and xenophobia, the debates that led to this commission normalized them. Many of those who came to testify at the commissions spoke about "the others." The gates of difference, of "us versus them" became wide open, they were never closed.

I hadn't lived in Quebec since 1998. My husband had found a job in Ottawa in the high-tech sector, and we moved. I missed Montreal terribly. I missed both the French language and the culture. My Muslim friends in Quebec would complain about how they had become, because of their hijabs, their names, or self-identification, pawns in this debate and how they constantly feared for the safety of themselves and their children.

In 2010, the Liberal government of premier Jean Charest introduced Bill 94, which (particularly targeting niqab) would have required people to uncover their faces to identify themselves before receiving any government services. According to a 2010 Angus Reid Public Opinion poll, the bill was supported by 95 per cent of Quebecers at the time. The legislation ultimately failed to pass when the Liberals were defeated in the 2012 election.

In 2012, after *le printemps érable* and the student rebellion against the PLQ and their tuition fee increase, Pauline Marois appeared as the saviour of the Parti Québécois. Her strategists believed they could be smarter than the ADQ, seeing how profitable the identity issue could be in terms of votes. In 2013, Marois, was elected as the first woman premier of Quebec, and taking a lesson from Mario Dumont's previous success, she continued on the path of identity politics.

Pauline Marois proposed the Charter of Values, or La Charte de la laïcité. It was portrayed by her and her government as a charter to fight women's oppression and promote gender equality. It was supposedly targeting the main religious symbols, described as "conspicuous" like the kirpan, the yarmulke, the cross (depending on its size and place), and of course the famous hijab. It wasn't a very well-kept secret that the Charter of Values had the aim of mainly targeting Muslim women who chose to wear the headscarf. Their increasing numbers in the streets, in daycare centres, as educators, at universities, and in the public spaces in general was apparently creating a malaise according to Bernard Drainville, the minister who initiated the Charter.[1] And so, in the name of gender equality, women wearing the niqab or the hijab would be fired from their jobs to preserve the secularism of society. What irony!

Despite the hundreds of thousands of comments from individuals and organizations opposing the Charter as well as the legal advice Bernard Drainville received about the Charter's constitutionality, he went ahead with his project. But beyond all the heated debates, and the misleading arguments used by the party, two phenomena became apparent: the widening social rift between mainstream society and ethnic groups; and a normalization of the hateful comments directed towards Muslim women and Islam, not only on social media but also by some media commentators and, of course, by Janette Bertrand, a famous public figure, portraying *a popular feminism*, who called those who wear the hijab as "manipulées" (manipulated) and proclaimed herself as the head of the "pro-Charter camp."[2]

Even after her brief passage as premier of Quebec and the failure of her project of "La Charte des Valeurs," the djinn had escaped the bottle, and the demonization of religious signs, and particularly the hijab and the women who wore it, became common.

When the PLQ won the election in 2014, the Charter of Values was buried, but the PLQ produced another legal chef d'oeuvre in Bill 62, which ended up targeting another tiny group: women wearing niqabs. Quebec's Bill 62 passed. It required people giving or receiving public services to do so with their faces uncovered—services such as taking the bus or borrowing a library book. Even though no one in Quebec could answer the very simple question, how many women actually wore the niqab in Quebec, politicians and media kept debating it.

In 2017, a survey showed that 76 per cent of Quebecers backed the law, and 24 per cent opposed it. But this opinion is not exclusive to Quebec. The same survey, conducted by Ipsos Public Affairs for Global News, found that 68 per cent of Canadian adults would either strongly or somewhat back the religious neutrality law in their part of the country. The legal banning of hijab and other religious symbols continued its way in Canada, bringing more scrutiny on Muslim women, their bodies, their clothes and their appearance. In 2011, former Canadian prime minister Stephen Harper formally introduced a ban on niqabs, or face veils, worn by women taking the Canadian citizenship oath. During his long reign, from 2006 until 2015, Stephen Harper introduced Bill 51, that became the new version of the Anti-Terrorism Act, the first one having been introduced by the Jean Chretien Liberal government in the aftermath of the September 11, 2001 attacks.

Not only did these anti-terrorism legislations effectively create a special legal status for Muslims and their incrimination under terrorism charges, it also broadened Islamophobia to reach women and the way they dress. Using the niqab, a complex religious garment worn by a minority of Muslim women that covers their entire face except the eyes, Stephen Harper wanted now to ride the Islamophobic wave to a new election victory in 2015. He hired for this purpose Lynton Crosbie, an Australian political strategist, known for his Islamophobic comments.

In 2012, the *Daily Mail* of London, UK reported, citing anonymous sources, that Crosbie had told Boris Johnson, then mayor of London (whose political advisor he was), to stop spending so much time on "f—— Muslims."[3]

It is fair to say that the majority of Canadians have never met or spoken to a Muslim woman wearing a niqab in their lives, but still they had a strong opinion against it. Natasha Bakht in her book *In Your Face: Law, Justice, and Niqab-Wearing Women in Canada* spoke to several Canadian women wearing niqab and concluded that all of them had decided to wear it out of their devotion to God and, in most cases, against the wishes and advice of their families. Her findings confirm what other studies, in France, Netherlands, and Australia, concluded about the meaning of niqab to most women who wear it.

Stephen Harper wanted to ban niqab during the citizenship ceremony. This issue almost hijacked the 2015 federal election campaign. "Are you with or against niqab?" was the question on the ballot, in a sort of a referendum. It didn't matter whether you voted Liberal, NDP, or Conservative, or if you were a man or a woman, a progressive or a conservative. Everyone had an opinion. And it was usually against the niqab.

Anne Kingston, the late Canadian award-winning journalist, described in one of her articles what the government of Stephen Harper managed to achieve.

> Shortly after its 2006 election, the government removed the word "equality" from the mandate of Status of Women Canada, a federal government organization formed to "promote equality for women and their full participation in the economic, social and democratic life of Canada" ("equality" was reinstated after protests). Cuts to the funding of that organization saw twelve of sixteen regional offices shuttered and the elimination of the $1-million Status of Women Independent Research Fund. Funding criteria were redrafted; dozens of women's service providers (including rape crisis centres) that engaged in advocacy or lobbying for law reform, became ineligible for funding or saw budgets slashed.[4]

Stephen Harper wouldn't have expected that a Muslim woman, Zunera Ishaq, would challenge his ban in court. In October 2015 she won her challenge in the Federal Court of Appeal. The Harper government took the case to the Supreme Court of Canada. The following month, the federal election was won by the Liberal government under Justin Trudeau, which almost immediately withdrew the federal challenge.

During that campaign a non-Muslim friend of mine approached me. She was adamant at resisting Prime Minister Harper's anti-niqab campaign, which was turning Canadians against each other. Together and with the help of another friend, we launched a website where Canadian women could sign their name to protest the use of "Niqab" in the federal campaign and the stigmatization of Muslim women. Hundreds of prominent Canadian women signed their names: university chancellors, professors, engineers, doctors. They were all against using the niqab as a wedge issue. Canadians weren't easily manipulated.

Derogatory comments about Muslim women became more frequent on social media, and Muslim women reported being harassed on the street. Of course, those who wore the niqab were the primary targets, but those in hijab were the collateral damage.

In 2018, François Legault was elected premier of Quebec. On the campaign trail, he promised to tackle the question of *laïcité* that his political predecessors had been unable to do. His Bill 21 became law and the first provincial legislation to ban religious symbols such as crosses, hijabs, turbans, and yarmulkes for people in public services. It is a legal ban that denies Muslim women the right to show her devotion to God wherever she desires.

This is how the new understanding of *laïcité* is applied. Instead of using it as a policy to ensure the government's neutrality and to prevent the domination of public institutions by any single religious tradition, the new *laïcité* suppresses selected minority religious traditions. The justification of this ban—gender equality and avoidance of proselytizing on behalf of any faith—is based on utter falsehood. Women wearing the hijab or even the niqab of their own free will are not a sign of gender inequality, nor are men wearing a kippa or men or women wearing a cross.

The new law is still under legal challenge in Quebec.

Islam, Islamophobia, and Women

How to write about Islamophobia without becoming a victim of my rhetoric; without turning into an anthropologist, a sociologist, or an Islamic legal scholar; without becoming an apologist for violence or abuse done under the name of Islam, by Muslims against Muslims or non-Muslims, men or women; and without being accused of denying any criticism of Islam and Muslims.

In 2004, I was invited to speak at a panel entitled "Is it necessary to cover with a veil Islamic affairs?" in Quebec City. After I spoke about the challenges I faced as a Muslim woman wearing a headscarf, one of the co-panelists turned to me and bluntly declared: "You have a choice: remove your headscarf and these challenges will disappear, so why do you want to keep martyrizing yourself, we are not in Saudi Arabia or Iran." It was a shocking reply but nevertheless, I think this woman spoke her mind, and I suspect that many others would have had similar reflections but were embarrassed to tell them to me upfront.

So why do I "martyrize" myself, while the solution is so simple: remove that "thing" from the top of my head and all my worries will be gone? First, what this co-panelist was referring to is a myth. I know many women, Muslims and non-Muslims, wearing hijab or not, facing challenges of racism and discrimination in the workplace, in schools, in public transportation. Discrimination exists with and without the hijab. The panelist's attitude was rude, not to say crude, coming from igno-rance and a position of "white privilege" that cannot be excused. This was a time when Black Lives Matter had not gained prominence and residential Indigenous schools were still to appear in the headlines.

In one of its report, Statistics Canada says that "Arab, Korean and West Asian women had the lowest employment rates among the visible minority groups. In 2006, the employment gap between Arab women and nonvisible minority women of core working age was 27.3 percentage points. For Korean women, the difference with nonvisible minority women was 23.5 points; for West Asian women, it was 21.7."

The report makes no reference to any religion.

Speaking and reflecting about my experiences as a Muslim woman wearing a hijab isn't about portraying myself as a martyr or a heroine. I don't want to suffer in order to reach Heaven. My spiritual journey started with a hijab, and so far I feel that it is part of my personality. Removing it would be hiding my true identity. Moreover, as long as my hijab is not banned from any public space, and is illegal in the country, why should I remove it in order to make others comfortable? The problem is surely with them.

Aren't we serious about fighting racism, homophobia, antisemitism, misogyny, xenophobia? Why do we accuse the victims and not the criminals? "You've created your own suffering" is pretty much the attitude often used when women are the victims of violence. For a rape survivor, it can be a revealing dress or "loose" behaviour that is the cause. If she hadn't gone out late at night or had "kept her knees together" (as an Alberta Federal Court Justice said to a sexual assault victim) she wouldn't have been raped. For me also, it is the way I am dressed that creates the discomfort that people feel when they justify discrimination against me. A friend of mine, born and raised in Ghana, when told to remove her hijab to better integrate, sarcastically replied, "Sure, I can remove my hijab, but how about my skin? Should I remove it, too?"

Similar attitudes prevail regarding domestic abuse. Many times, while growing up in Tunisia and later even in Canada, I heard women being told to "shut up" or "be nicer" so their husbands wouldn't beat them or abuse them. Yes, our societies do justify violence against women. By saying "men will be men" and "boys will be boys" we normalize violence against women. And consequently, "women should be women" means they should talk less and suck it up. Therefore, in order for me to be a good woman, and according to the logic of my co-panelist who, for the record, is an outspoken feminist, I should suck it up. I should respond to my "oppression" by liberating myself from own oppression: my hijab.

According to this logic, it is *I* who am the problem. I choose my own torments. At least this logic gives me a certain agency: I can make choices. But my choices aren't right. They lead to my victimization. The only choice for me that would be salvatory is to remove my hijab—or in other circumstances, in the abusers' words, to "go back to your own country!"

Hijab became the apology for whatever looks bad in Islam. Wearing my hijab, I have to be defending honour-killing of daughters, polygyny, and terrorism. My belief in Islam first and then my donning of hijab makes me *illico presto* responsible for every act of violence conducted by Muslim extremists in the name of God and justified by their own readings and interpretations of religious texts.

This attitude is at the heart of Islamophobia. Calling me to explain all the patriarchal oppression around the world because of my hijab is Islamophobia. Calling me to explain violence in Muslim countries and ignoring or not understanding that violence takes place everywhere regardless of religion or race is Islamophobia. Singling me out to denounce terrorism, forced marriage, female genital mutilation, honour-killing, etc. just because I am a Muslim woman is also a flagrant sign of Islamophobia.

Now I will attempt to tackle these issues without feeling that I am responsible for them because I am a Muslim. Many times, while talking about these difficult issues, I have found myself on the defensive, trying to justify some "Islamic behaviour" or trying to allay the insecurity that these questions might cause. My opinions here are personal and as a Muslim who has read and thought about these issues.

Polygyny

In Islam polygyny is allowed. A man can marry up to four wives at the same time with the strict condition that he be able to support them equally and have permission from his wife or wives to remarry. However, polygyny is not a pillar of Islam. It isn't a religious duty, like praying or fasting or giving charity. It is only a permit for special circumstances. There are many writings by Muslims about polygyny, defending the practice or opposing it. Some Muslim countries, like Tunisia and Turkey, have banned the practice, other countries, like Morocco and Malaysia, apply certain conditions. And several other Muslim countries, including Saudi Arabia and Libya, allow it.

I didn't grow up in an environment where polygyny was practiced. I didn't see its consequences. While I was on a literary trip to Senegal, I was struck by a comment made by a Senegalese woman about polygyny and how it ruined many families with children from late marriages (by men): children grown up not knowing or having time with their old father; complex inheritance issues involving spouses and numerous children; the emotional drain due to constant squabbles. This picture only confirmed my view against the practice.

Polygyny is one of the easiest religious issues that Muslim reformers could agree on. But unfortunately, the majority of scholars are men, with a possible personal interest, and sometimes women are willing to be a second or third wife for personal advantages. The younger wives obviously get the most attention.

In my opinion, polygyny should not be seen from the religious point of view but rather from social, legal, cultural, and economic perspectives.

Honour Killing and Genital Mutilation

The only thing I would say about these two horrible and violent topics is that they are religiously, legally, and morally wrong. There is no justification for them whatsoever. Deliberately associating them directly or indirectly to any religion is wrong.

Gendered Islamophobia in Numbers

In 2017, the year of the shooting at the Quebec City Mosque, there were 349 incidents of police-reported hate crimes against Muslims in Canada. That was a jump of 151 per cent from the previous year, which saw 139 such reports. However, the majority of hate crimes in Canada, about two-thirds, go unreported.

Year	2014	2015	2016	2017	2018	2019	2020	2021
Police reported crimes against Muslims	99	159	139	349	173	102	84	144

Sources: Statistics Canada, *Middle East Eye*

It is surely significant that of all minority and immigrant groups, Muslims have been the main victims of hate-motivated crimes in Montreal; in the first part of 2019, nearly 60 per cent of all hate crimes were targeted towards them. It should be noted that reports do not identify the exact number of women affected by this violence. In July 2021, Fatema Abdalla of the National Council of Canadian Muslims reported that at least fifteen attacks on Muslim women had been reported in the cities of Edmonton and Calgary over the previous six months. A study, conducted between May and June 2022, by the Association for Canadian Studies on the impact of Quebec's discriminatory Bill 21, reported that within Jewish, Sikh, and Muslim communities there was an overall decline in feeling accepted as full-fledged members of Quebec society; of those women surveyed, 80 per cent did not feel accepted.

Below is a list of crimes against Muslim women that recently received prominence in the media. But violence is not abstract or a mere statistic to be studied; it is real, against a person, and traumatic. The trauma and terror the victims suffer can be gauged from the examples given below. All the women cited here, and others, will carry the scars from their attacks for their lifetimes.

> » October 24, 2022, Montreal North saw three hate incidents targeting women wearing a hijab. In two of them, the women were verbally abused while in their cars and the third one occurred in the workplace.

> » June 23, 2021, two women were walking near Alderwood Park in Edmonton, when a man wearing a mask started yelling racial remarks at them. He grabbed one woman by her hijab and pushed her to the ground, knocking her unconscious. He then pulled out a knife, knocked the second female to the ground, and held her down with his knife at her throat. He then ran off. The first woman regained consciousness and was transported to hospital by an ambulance. The second woman sustained minor injuries.

> » June 11, 2021, in Edmonton, a Black Muslim woman in her fifties was out for a walk when an attacker approached her from behind and threw her onto the pavement.

> » February 17, 2021, a Muslim woman who was waiting for a bus at an LRT Station in Edmonton was approached by a stranger. He made a fist and swore at her, threatening to physically assault and kill her. In an interview with CBC News, the woman said, "I'm dealing with two sets of traumas . . . I am dealing with the trauma of the attack and I'm dealing with the trauma that the Edmonton Police Services officer I called kindly rejected me."

» December 16, 2020, in Edmonton, a young Black Muslim woman was attacked at the Southgate LRT station. She is the third Black Muslim woman to be attacked in the daytime in that area. The suspect, Rene Ladoucer, thirty-two, was arrested and charged with assault.

» Around December 9, 2020, two Black Muslim women, a mother and her daughter, were attacked near the parking lot of South Edmonton Mall. The man shouted racial obscenities and shattered a window of their car. He physically assaulted them when they came out of their car. Both women were thrown to the ground. The attacker ripped off the mother's hijab, using the N-word, and told them to "go back to your country."

These Edmonton attacks are somewhat surprising, given that Muslims have been in the area for more than a century, and the city boasts the oldest mosque in Canada.

It is hard to deny that the violence against Muslim women—for example the attacks on Muslim Black women in Alberta and the attacks on the mosques and visible Muslims on the streets—has directly followed from the Islamophobic atmosphere that preceded the legal banning of religious symbols, including the hijab and the niqab, with Bill 21 in Quebec and the federal legislation of the Harper government. The so-called "war on terror" and President Trump's inflammatory speeches only added to the toxic atmosphere. Sometimes even crimes committed by Muslims—for example the killings of three young women and a relative by the parents and their son near Kingston— became easily stereotyped as typical Muslim behaviour.

The COVID-19 pandemic and the rise of the far-right extremism

At the height of the 2020-21 pandemic, social media hosted an explosion of anti-Muslim and anti-immigrant misinformation and hate-filled rhetoric. Postings such as "Muslims are super spreaders of the Coronavirus"[1] or "Mosques are hotbeds for outbreaks"[2] added to the already existent misconceptions and ignorant statements about Muslims and Islam. On April 24, 2020, at the beginning of Ramadan, and a few weeks after the beginnings of the lockdowns in many Canadian provinces, a man recorded himself on social media in front of the Al Rashid Mosque in Edmonton, the oldest Mosque in Canada, with the message: "So it's April 24th—the start of the Ramadan bombathon, and I'm just performing my civic duty to make sure that no one's actually showing up at the Al Rashid Mosque."[3]

The pandemic didn't create this hateful environment, it only enhanced it. In their report *Online Environmental Scan of Right-Wing Extremism in Canada*, Jacob Davey, Cécile Guerin, and Mackenzie Hart note that the "global pattern—acts of terrorism committed by the far-right—have increased by 320 per cent over the past five years, supported by an increasingly connected and internationalist community of right-wing extremism. Canada has not been isolated from this trend and in recent years the number of hate groups operating in the country has tripled." Most of the hate groups are known to have antisemitism and Islamophobia on their agendas.

Quebec's Bill 21: "An Act Respecting the Laicity of the State"

Justice Femme, a Montreal-based organization that offers legal and psychological support to women, has said that in the months after Bill 21 (which bars public school teachers and public servants in position of authority from wearing religious symbols including the hijab in the case of Muslim women) was tabled in Quebec's National Assembly in March 2019, it had received more than forty calls from hijab-wearing women. According to Justice Femme, the women who called reported a wide range of incidents, from aggressive comments to physical violence. These include:

» Four cases of physical assault in public, including two attempts to rip the hijab off and one of being spat at.

» Six cases of harassment and intimidation at work.

» More than a dozen cases of cyber-bullying, prompting

several women to remove profile photos featuring their hijab.

For instance, on May 15, 2019, Fatima Ahmad was attacked outside the Charlevoix Metro station. She says a man approached her "and then he hit me with his hand on my chest and he pulled my niqab." She filed a report with Montreal police.

The Niqab Issue (2015)

» In 2015, Zunera Ishaq, a Pakistani who lived with her family in Canada, was prevented by Stephen Harper's government to take her citizenship oath while wearing her niqab, a face cover worn by a minority of Muslim women. She legally challenged this ban in the courts and later she won.

» October 4, 2015, Safira Merriman, a French Canadian pregnant woman wearing a niqab, was assaulted in Fairview Mall, Toronto, during a period when prime minister Stephen Harper's anti-niqab speeches had created a negative atmosphere.

The Quebec Charter of Values (2013, 2014)

» January 13, 2014, Sama Al-Obaidy reported being attacked in the Montreal metro. "A lady came up and tried to remove my hijab forcefully," Al-Obaidy said. "She told me my hijab and myself don't belong in Quebec and after a few exchanges of words she decided to start pulling on my veil. I had to eventually stop her."[4]

» January 2014, a forty-seven-year-old Muslim woman, Naima Rharouity, died in an accident in the escalator at the Fabre Metro station in Montreal. It was impossible to know if her hijab was caught, causing her to fall, but the media fed on it: "Strangled by her hijab"; "Where was Allah?" "One less terrorist in Quebec." Readers expressed hope that this incident would teach Muslims a lesson.[5]

» On September 2, 2013, in Sainte-Foy, Quebec, a Muslim woman wearing hijab and her family were assaulted by a female assailant in a shopping mall. The assailant approached the women in the mall and started to insult her and tell her to change her religion. An altercation ensued and the police were called.

What motivates these acts of violence against women? Legal scholar and journalist Azeezah Kanji links such attacks to a "product of a much broader context of structural Islamophobia." They are a result of "state-sponsored practices of draconian counter-terrorism measures," such as surveillance of Muslims and laws like the Zero Tolerance for Barbaric Cultural Practices Act, and the hijab ban in Quebec (Bill 21). "All of which produce a climate in which people think it's normal to think of Muslim life as demonized and devalued."[6]

I couldn't agree more.

A report published in May-June 2022 gave the results of a survey of opinions, perceptions and experiences of a representative sample of 1,828 Quebecers, including 632 Muslims, 165 Jews, and 56 Sikhs. According to the report, there was "severe social stigmatization of Muslim women, marginalization of Muslim women and very disturbing declines in their sense of well-being, their ability to fulfil their aspirations, sense of safety, but also hope for the future."[7] Furthermore, "[f]orty-seven per cent of Muslim women said they'd been treated unfairly by a person in a position of authority . . . Two thirds of Muslim women said they'd been a victim of and/or a witness to a hate crime. Seventy-three per cent said their feeling of being safe in public had worsened."

The current Islamophobic climate according to the conclusions of this report, is not the immediate result of the introduction and implementation of Bill 21. Prejudicial attitudes have been gestating in Quebec for nearly twenty years, when the debate over so-called "reasonable accommodations" for religious minorities first took hold.

Another troubling conclusion of this report is that only 40 per cent of people surveyed believe a public servant who does not comply with the law should lose their job. As if people want this law implemented to give them a false sense of security. As if deep down they believe that Bill 21 is discriminatory but they still "support" it to feel that their "identity" is safe.

One positive and optimistic observation in this report is that younger women, who are more exposed to Muslims in all walks of life, are less likely to be prejudiced against Muslims. Just 31 per cent of women aged 18-24 support Bill 21.

The Multiple Layers of Hate

I have never been physically abused because of my faith. But during my thirty years in Canada, I have been exposed to threatening gestures, verbal abuse, including obscenities, intimidating stares, and spitting. They were sporadic and random occurrences; I didn't link them to any public event or provocation from me or somewhere else. I have found them banal and indicative of the normalization of verbal abuse directed towards women on social media. Obviously, mainstream society is unwilling to entertain this racist image of itself. All well and good.

What I found harder to explain and counterintuitive is that the idea of gendered Islamophobia was dismissed even by many Muslims. I was once on a panel with other Muslim women, all from immigrant backgrounds but with different relationships with Islam. We all agreed that we faced racism at different levels based on our names, skin shades, and religion. But we were heavily criticized by some people in the audience, who saw in our presentation only ingratitude of the "welcoming Canadian society."

According to this view, as a good Muslim immigrant, I should never criticize the country that welcomed me, and saved me from poverty or oppression or whatever other reason led me to leave my country of origin. Muslim immigrants, they believe furthermore, are responsible for their situation. Their unemployment is due to laziness or lack of initiative. The discrimination they face originates from their stubbornness in keeping to the backward traditions and ways that they came with.

This is nothing but internalized colonialism and Islamophobia. Rania Rizvi a Canadian Muslim student at Rutgers University, describes this syndrome eloquently: "In their pursuit of the 'American Dream,' my parents hid their Muslim identities and became upstanding citizens of the Western world. They kept their heads down, obeyed the law, and quietly blended into the crowd of Hindu Indians, biting down their ancestors' tongue when they spoke." She explained how "Islamophobia became learning to laugh instead of fighting back. It became staring at the name tag on your desk after recess and wondering why your parents couldn't pick a name that sounded 'less Muslim.'"[1]

At the session I have described above, one of the panelists rightfully responded that "constructive criticism is a sign of belonging. What better example of a civic and democratic engagement than participation in the public debate with observations, feedbacks, and most of all a call for accountability." We have come to a democracy, I would add, there is a constitution that defends the rights of all citizens. We did not come here to accept oppression and abuse.

Unfortunately, many Muslims feel that despite Islamophobia in mainstream society, it is better to keep a low profile and avoid confrontation. "If you don't talk about it then one day it will somehow disappear." Would we accept antisemitism or racism the same way? Surely not. The recent Black Lives Matter protests showed that people are not willing to accept abuse, of whatever nature. I have chosen to speak about Islamophobia and in particular that variety directed at Muslim women because I believe that I should call it out.

Many times, while writing this book, I found myself unable to go on. The subject is too close to the bone. In 2017, when a gunman killed six men and injured nineteen others in Quebec City Mosque, for the first time I was frightened and feeling unsafe in Canada. The same feeling overcame me when I heard the tragic news of the killing of four members of a Muslim family in London, Ontario in 2021. The grandmother, the mother, the father, and the daughter were killed, leaving a nine-year-old boy orphaned. A pickup driver had decided to mow into them simply because of their Islamic faith.

Fears about my safety had always been hidden and suppressed. It took violent events like these for them to surface.

The perpetrators of personal attacks against me have been both men and women. I don't want to indulge in caricatures and simplistic generalizations. However, my observation is that men's behaviours have been patronizing, whereas for women my Islamic "visibility" appears as a threat. One woman in Vancouver refused to take the elevator with me, saying that my hijab told her that I was a terrorist; none of the people observing us said a word to protest against that racist rant. In another instance a woman with a man closed an entrance door to my face, because she said I looked suspicious. Ironically, I remembered how many times I patiently held the door to people behind me, never thought to assess how suspicious or dangerous they looked.

By trying to eliminate me or my physical presence these individuals display an underlying superiority about how they dress and how they think about me. This is how I imagine these women think of me:

» Hijab is a tool that banalizes women's oppression.

» A woman in hijab relegates women's struggles to the garbage bin and encourages misogyny.

And this is how I imagine men think of me:

» She is an oppressed woman. I can oppress her too.

» She is a passive woman so I can straighten her out without consequences.

When women attack me, it is the insecurity they feel about themselves that they project on me, or a sense of superiority because their own choices are better their mine. When men attack me, it is the sexual male superiority and the right to colonize the bodies of women, who are perceived as inferior or sexually repressed because of their gender and ethnicity.

Of course, we all have preconceptions about other people.

One day, while crossing a street in downtown Ottawa, I saw a young woman with purple hair, piercings all over her body, and tattoos on her arms and legs. She made me uncomfortable. I thought she was perhaps another lost soul and perhaps needs help. But surprisingly she smiled at me and wished me "Eid Mubarak." This was one of my humblest moments. I felt guilty about my feeling of moral superiority that she so quickly overturned with two words of greeting, "Eid Mubarak"; this young woman happened to know that it was the time of the Islamic festival of Eid. Perhaps she had Muslim friends, or was even herself a Muslim. I should have stopped to talk with her. But such moments pass too quickly. She showed me, however, how wrong we can be in our preconceptions.

But there is a big difference between holding negative preconceptions and acting upon them. It is the latter that leads to racist acts. The former hurts and consumes our inner soul. Both are wrong, but to different degrees.

Education is important. It is crucial, but it is not the sole key to eradicating Islamophobia, antisemitism, and racism from our lives. We need something bigger. We need to tackle not only the minds but also the systems that brought us racism.

A new social contract is needed. A covenant agreed upon by everyone. Not only the victims, not only the aggressors, not only the police, not only the politicians. This contract should be shaped around values of compassion and justice. Both are crucial values in moving forward together. When the first Europeans arrived at the shores of Turtle Island, the First Nations people welcomed them. They helped them find food, find their way, and care for their sick. These are positive values that we should teach to our kids in schools and reflect upon in our lives.

But we also need an honest re-examination of the past. An admission of the harm caused by European powers that colonized America, Africa, Asia, and the Middle East, directly impacting the fates of indigenous men and women in those lands. For instance, using the pretext of "liberating" and "educating" "Moslem" women, British and French colonial governments, by imposing their alien educational and judicial systems, destroyed or crippled the very structures that had protected local women. It is not that the status of women was necessarily better than of their European counterparts, it is simply that the occupation of their lands worsened the condition of indigenous women. Moreover, the prospect of foreign soldiers harassing local women going outside—to the market, to the fields, or to visit their relatives—gave more reasons for patriarchal societies to control their women.

In the nineteenth century, during the British occupation of Egypt, Lord Cromer pronounced that the British had come to bring education to the "Mohametan" women and girls; however, the cost of education only increased, and many young girls were not sent to school for that reason. Ironically, Lord Cromer, after he returned to Britain, became one of the fiercest opponents of the suffragette movement for British women's rights.

In 2002, when the United States invaded Afghanistan, the second most publicly pronounced motive for that invasion, besides going after the terrorists, was to help Afghan women to go to schools and get rid of the burka. Overnight, everyone became a feminist, and even the staunch conservatives who were against stem-cell research and abortion joined the chorus of voices to "liberate" Afghan women.

Laura Bush, the wife of American president George W Bush, went on television to speak in favour of the war, which she said was to "liberate women from the burqa" and explain how Afghan women were tortured for wearing nail polish.[2] The war ended up killing hundreds of thousands of Afghans and created numerous thousands of refugees. It was the same George Bush who on his first day in the Oval Office cut off funding to any international family-planning organizations that offered abortion services or counselling. In 2003 George Bush renamed January 22—the anniversary of the Roe vs Wade decision allowing abortion on demand—as the National Sanctity of Human Life Day and compared abortion to terrorism.

When President Joe Biden announced American troop withdrawal from Afghanistan after twenty years of war and occupation, George Bush made a rare public criticism, once again hiding behind a concern for Muslim women: "I'm afraid Afghan women and girls are going to suffer unspeakable harm."[3] The reality was that in those two decades of war, Afghan women became victims of US bombings of civil gathering like weddings (apparently in error) and the killings of villagers by US soldiers and Afghan warlords.

Malalai Joya, Afghan politician and feminist, has described the effect of this hypocrisy on the plight of Afghan women in these terms:

"Unfortunately, they pushed us from the frying pan into the fire as they replaced the barbaric regime of the Taliban with the misogynist warlords."[4]

In her brilliant book, *Do Muslim Women Need Saving?* Lila Abu-Lughod tackles this issue at length, saying that liberating women abroad isn't a simple matter of removing the veil or the burka but rather it is a complex process that goes beyond any type of clothing and involves creating socioeconomic opportunities that are most of the times lacking because of economic globalization, patriarchy, oppressive political regimes (often supported by the West), and economic conditions.

Muslim women are "oppressed" not through their dressing but through their economic conditions, which are beyond their control or the control of organizations that try to "liberate" them. Sometimes women find their liberation in what seems from a distance to be oppressive. In many poor neighbourhoods in Tunis or Cairo, religious schools became for some women the only way to leave the house, get a good secular and religious education, and eventually find a job or a volunteer position and be able to teach other women. They feel needed and appreciated. It is their own liberation.

What all women long for is to be able to choose. Choice isn't an easy thing. It comes with the privilege of eating properly, having security and having a job.

Today, we need Muslim women to be able to make their own choices. Even when these choices are not what we desire for ourselves.

Systemic Islamophobia or a Few Bad Apples?

In 2017, in the aftermath of the Quebec City mosque shooting, a Liberal MP, Iqra Khalid, presented a motion that called on the Canadian government to recognize the "increasing climate of hate and fear," to condemn Islamophobia and other forms of systemic racism and religious discrimination, to undertake a study to help the Canadian government better understand Islamophobia, collect data and come up with strategies and recommendations to combat and eliminate it "with a holistic response through evidence-based policy-making."[1]

Some Conservative MPs and media commentators, however, objected to the term "Islamophobia." But the disagreement didn't focus only on the word, it went further. The opponents claimed that the term was an exaggerated description of some "sad" incidents, which were the work of a "few bad apples," and if Canada went ahead and acknowledged the existence of Islamophobia, it would curtail freedom of expression and perhaps give a back-door entry to blasphemy laws.

The motion, M-103, despite its nonbinding aspect, did not pass. It gave rise to a divisive and unproductive debate. Unfortunately, the Liberals, who had a political majority at that time, did not support the bill and in my opinion threw Iqra Khalid and her motion under the bus. She ended up receiving hundreds of hate messages during the process. It was a wasted opportunity for Canada to do better.

The next year, the parliamentary Standing Committee on Canadian Heritage held hearings about "Taking action against systematic racism and religious discrimination including Islamophobia" and released its final report. It included thirty recommendations, like creating national standards for reporting hate crimes, developing policy and research on racism, and boosting government support for cross-cultural programs but only two out of these thirty recommendations explicitly mentioned Islamophobia. It recommended that the federal government declare January 29 as a day of action against Islamophobia (which was accepted by the government years later). But there was no recommendation on how to combat it in the media, in Canadian institutions, and in the streets.

Is the use of the word *Islamophobia* an exaggerated response to a few unfortunate incidents or is there something systemic going on?

In September 2020, a Muslim volunteer security guard at a mosque in the Rexdale neighbourhood of Toronto was killed while sitting on a chair near the mosque. The Canadian Anti-Hate Network, an organization that monitors and reports on hate groups, says it linked the accused's social media activity to neo-Nazi ideology.

CBC News has confirmed that the killer followed at least one such Facebook group, had a Nazi symbol on his Instagram account, and had posted a chant on YouTube linked to a hate cult.

The victim, Mohamed-Aslim Zafis, fifty-four years old, had his throat slit. His family decided to make camera footage of the killing public, to convince it of the seriousness of the crime. According to Toronto police, another man, Rampreet (Peter) Singh, thirty-nine, was also fatality stabbed on September 7, five kilometres from where Zafis was slain days later. The police could not "exclude that possibility" that the two killings were connected.[2]

What was troubling here was the police unwillingness to investigate these killings as hate crime, despite clear indications.

One year after Zafis's killing, during a food drive at the Rexdale Mosque to honour his legacy, his daughter, Bebi Zafis, pronounced, "I'm afraid to go to mosque, to wear a hijab, to go out there. I'm not the next victim but sometimes I feel I am." The killer was found on March 2023 "not criminally responsible," raising, once again the possibility that hate crimes are hard to prove or even denied when the victims belong to marginalized communities.

It isn't a secret that white supremacists form a credible domestic threat to the national security of Canada.

A 2015 report stated that there were at least one hundred white supremacist and neo-Nazi groups active in Canada, as well as roughly 30,000 individuals involved with "sovereign citizen" philosophies that typically reject Canadian laws. In an interview, one of the authors of the report, Barbara Perry, described how these far-right groups target different communities including Muslims:

> Historically, the emphasis was on antisemitism and anti-black rhetoric. In Canada, that was also accompanied by anti-Indigenous sentiment and attacks on Indigenous communities as well. But it changes and shifts over time, depending on the target *du jour*, so in recent years we have seen an interesting shift. I wouldn't say that antisemitism or anti-black rhetoric or anti-Indigenous sentiments have been replaced, but they have been supplemented by a renewed focus or perhaps a new focus on Islam, which is really the target of the animosity of many of the far-right groups in Canada.[3]

But despite this and other information, on January 31, 2019, two days after the second anniversary of the Quebec City Mosque tragedy, Premier Francois Legault declared that "I don't think there is Islamophobia in Quebec." Later he changed his position by saying that discrimination exists but was not systemic or widespread.[4]

There has been no initiative from the police to increase their patrols around the mosques. It took the Toronto police three days to make an arrest in the murder of Mohamed-Aslim Zafis. There has also been no serious attempt from politicians to harden the hate speech laws.

In Alberta, there were calls by some Muslim advocates to include the "Three Percenters," a US-based right-wing, antigovernment militia also active in Canada, as a "terrorist organization." It didn't happen until later.

In 2020, when Prime Minister Justin Trudeau was asked whether there would be a national strategy to combat the rise of white supremacy groups in Canada, he kept repeating the same banalities: "We put in place years ago more funding to assure the security of the vulnerable places of worships . . . "[5]

These funds to help security for places of worship are problematic on three levels:

> » Small, racialized communities often don't have the knowledge or experience to deal with government bureaucracy to procure funds. Often also the members are new immigrants with poor language skills. Surely, they should not be put at risk for these reasons?

> » The onus is on the victims to protect themselves and their places of worship. One would expect the government to protect them as they do other citizens.

> » The increased funding concept is a reactive concept. What is really needed is a proactive and pre-emptive strategy.

It took the federal government four years of sidelining the Islamophobia question (the Quebec City Mosque attack in 2017), a minority government, a spectacular, scary, and embarrassing "insurrection" on Capitol Hill by far-right groups, and many years of pleading by human rights organizations before January 29 was declared as an action day against Islamophobia.

We had to wait until June 6, 2021 after the tragic killing of a Muslim family in London, Ontario to finally see the narrative of a "few bad apples" put to rest. The family were visibly Muslim by their garb. Only then did the Canadian government start publicly to admit the existence of "systemic Islamophobia" in Canada.

The tragedy created a "mea culpa" moment for several Conservative MPs who had previously either flatly denied the existence of Islamophobia or participated in inflaming the climate of Islamophobia after 9/11. Michelle Rempel Garner was the first in her party to publicly say that her party's proposed niqab ban (Motion M-103) during the 2015 campaign trail was "wrong." Tim Uppal, then Minister of

Multiculturalism, also regrated his role in supporting that legislation and admitted that "it alienated Muslim Canadians." Several other MPs who voted against M-103 came out and regretted their "mistakes." Whether the "regrets" and "feeling sorry" were genuine or simply political expediency one cannot say. But they are strong admissions and clear evidence that there is a strong link between political bigotry and Islamophobic impact on the ground.

Quebec Premier Francois Legault, whose government passed Bill 21, the Laicity Act, has some serious self-reflection to do. Hiding behind noble principles such as gender equality and religious neutrality should never be an excuse to discriminate against women to pursue their dreams and pursue their dream jobs.

Following the London, Ontario killings, the Canadian government held a summit on Islamophobia in July 2021. After sitting on the fence and doing almost nothing about the dangerous propagation of hate speech and hate crimes, the government proposed to introduce new legislation to protect Canadians from hate speech and online harm. Violent white supremacist groups, like the Three Percenters, were finally added on June 25, 2021 to the list of terrorist organizations. The federal government expressed its commitment to appoint a special representative on combatting Islamophobia.

But when journalist and human rights activist Amira Elghawaby, a Muslim Canadian wearing a hijab, was appointed by Prime Minister Trudeau in January 2023 to fill this position, politicians in Quebec demanded the appointment to be rescinded because of comments she had made in a 2019 opinion piece.

The column, which she co-wrote with Bernie Farber, former member of the Canadian Jewish Congress, cited polling data to say that "a majority of Quebecers" who supported Bill 21 also held anti-Muslim views. As if any criticism of Bill 21 was a blasphemy.

In recent times there is a strong desire among people to bring about change. So even if politicians are not sincere or slow to respond to demands, there are many grass-roots movements working to bring about change. Alliances and networks are being formed for this purpose. On July 9, 2021, seventy-five imams across Canada offered

condolences and expressed solidarity with Indigenous people following the discoveries of unmarked graves at the sites of former residential schools. This solidarity and broader consciousness are surely to
be applauded. Similarly, the Union of British Columbia Indian Chiefs
(UBCIC) condemned with strong words the attack on the Muslim
family in London, Ontario. Many other organizations across the country, from different traditions and background did likewise. The Ontario
branch of the Rabbinical Assembly, the association for Conservative
rabbis, condemned the "atrocious attack on our Muslim brothers and
sisters," and affirmed its commitment to work with leaders "of all faiths
so that no Canadian will practice their religion in fear of intimidation
or violence."[6]

Colonialism and Women

In an essay entitled "Algeria Unveiled," Frantz Fanon reported on an exchange among officials of the French colonial administration concerning Algerians. He quoted, "If we want to strike Algerian society in its structure, in its faculty of resistance, we first have to conquer its women, we have to look for them behind their veils, where they hide themselves and in their house, where the men hide them."

This was not a simple and harmless opinion passing among French bureaucrats and military officials, it was the policy that was being implemented in colonial Algeria since 1830 by France. The policy targeting women, seen as the carriers of the Algerian culture, was simultaneously accompanied on the ground by tanks and guns targeting the men. It was only in 1962 that Algeria gained its independence from France, after a long and brutal war. The fate of Algerian women under French colonialism may be unknown to the majority of Canadians. But one should remember that women all around the world pay with their bodies and lives the costs of the colonization initiated by men.

In Turtle Island, the first settlers, French and British, adopted policies of colonization that were used similarly against other nations in Africa and Asia: brutal wars, erasure of Indigenous culture, shaming of Indigenous languages, and the removal of children from their families.

It took the white establishment more than a century to admit the wrongs committed by colonization. The road to justice is still long. In May 2019, the National Inquiry into Missing and Murdered Indigenous

Women and Girls in Canada, brought out its long-awaited report. Already in 2004, Amnesty International Canada had called the disappeared and murdered Indigenous women the "Stolen Sisters."

In 2014, the RCMP reported that the number of indigenous women and girls who had disappeared or been murdered was 1,181.

The report actually speaks of thousands of women with similar fates. We will never know exactly how many. The report also states that Indigenous women and girls were "twelve times more likely to be murdered or to go missing than members of any other demographic group in Canada and sixteen times more likely to be slain or disappear than white women." Commenting on the findings of these reports, Elder Albert McLeod, co-chair of the Manitoba Missing and Murdered Indigenous Women and Girls Coalition, said, "They're not specifically only for Indigenous people to understand, but it's for Canadians to understand the impact of colonization and how it has affected the Indigenous peoples."[1]

Despite the cultural and geographic differences between Algerian women and Indigenous women, both groups were victims of brutal and ruthless colonial administrations. Both groups were abused by police officers; both have seen their native languages banned from being taught at homes and in schools. Under the pretext of liberating women from the oppression of their male relatives and welcoming them into the world of civilization and legal rights, many Algerian women were forced to remove their veils. Their religion, Islam, was identified by the French colonial institutions as the main source of their oppression and backwardness. Many Algerians grew up not learning Arabic or ashamed speaking it.

In the case of Indigenous women, many of them who were fleeing domestic violence in their communities (another product of colonialism and difficult economic factors) were taken advantage of by either police officers or on the road by white men to be raped and killed.

France has never admitted its war crimes in Algeria. The word *genocide* was never pronounced by French politicians, despite the documented massacre committed by its forces. Even President Macron, during his pre-election campaign in 2017, in an interview with an Algerian television channel, called France's 132-year colonization of

Algeria a "crime against humanity."[2] But he forgot his words after the election. In 2021, the office of President Macron insisted on "no repentance nor apologies" as a line of conduct with its Algerian past colony.[3]

The Canadian Truth and Reconciliation Commission (TRC) of 2015 adopted the term *cultural genocide*, for the treatment of Indigenous people in this country. (The same term would apply elsewhere in the Americas.) It made ninety-four "calls to action." The Commission's report says that "The intent of the government's policy . . . was to assimilate Aboriginal people into broader Canadian society . . . At the end of this process, Aboriginal people were expected to have ceased to exist as a distinct people with their own governments, cultures and identities."

What does colonialism have to do with Islamophobia and violence against Muslim women? My argument is simple: colonialism was motivated by inherent racism, an ideology that assumes that the European races were superior to other races and were thus invested with a mission to civilize them.

In 1883, Canada's first prime minister, Sir John A Macdonald, told the House of Commons that residential schools would be one of the main weapons used against the "savage" in the native peoples. In a speech quoted by the TRC report, John A Macdonald said, "When the school is on the reserve the child lives with its parents, who are savages, he is surrounded by savages, and though he may learn to read and write his habits and training and mode of thought are Indian . . . He is simply a savage that can read and write."[4]

At about the same time in Egypt, another colonial project was in progress under Lord Cromer, the Consul General during the British occupation of Egypt between 1877 and 1907. In his book, *Modern Egypt*, Cromer wrote:

> It is absurd to suppose Europe will look on as a passive spectator whilst the retrograde government based on purely Muhammadan principles and oriental ideas [i.e. Islam], is established in Egypt. The material interests at stake are too important . . . the new generation of Egyptian has to be persuaded or forced into imbibing the true spirit of Western civilisation.[5]

> The position of women in Egypt, and Mohammedan coun-
> tries generally, is, therefore a fatal obstacle to the attainment
> of that elevation of thought and character which should
> accompany the introduction of Western civilisation.

During his time in Egypt, he initiated unveiling campaigns. Leila
Ahmed and Edward Said have written about the extent of damage Lord
Cromer's policies did to the local populations and in particular to women.

The ideas of Lord Cromer regarding Arab Muslim women are
not very different from those of Maurice Viollette, who served as
Governor General of Algeria between 1925 to 1927. According to him,
"One cannot envisage the question of relations between Europeans and
natives without devoting a special chapter to the native woman."

According to Jyhène Kebsi, Director of Learning and Teaching at
Macquarie University, Sydney, Australia, Viollette's stance finds its
parallel in the position of the current French president, who said that
"reforming" Islam necessitates a "reform" of Muslim women's life-
styles, including clothing.

Today when I hear about any Muslim being attacked in Canada, I
can't stop drawing links with being murdered and disappeared in the
Highway of Tears. I can't stop making links with Algerian, Tunisian,
and Egyptian women who decades ago were forced to remove their
veils by the colonizing powers.

I can't stop making links between the Indigenous children who were
separated from their families and forcibly sent to residential schools to
forget their languages and family traditions and the Algerian children
who were forced to learn French because the French banned Arabic
in primary school, dismissing it as backward. Describing the colonial
policies in Algeria, Malika Rahal, a French Algerian historian, writes:

> Classical Arabic language was in fact one of the first vic-
> tims of colonization: under colonial rule, there was no
> equivalent to the universities of the Qarawiyyin in Fes
> (Morocco) or the Zaytuna in Tunis. The establishment of
> schools with Arabic as a language of instruction was sub-
> ject to various types of bureaucratic hurdles and permis-
> sions that, de facto, made it impossible."[6]

Hijabization As Fashion

When I started to wear hijab in the early 1990s in Tunis, the "hijab peak" had not yet arrived. Few women in the larger cities or from the middle- and upper-class families wore the headscarf. It took a decade to see the trend spread. There are many reasons for this. First, the influence of religious programing broadcast on satellite from the Gulf countries; second, the influence of the "tele-Quranist" Amr Khaled; and third, widespread sexual harassment in the streets of Muslims countries. To add to these, there arose the re-emergence and reassertion of Muslim identity after many decades of political and social repression in countries like Tunisia and Turkey, where the headscarf had been demonized as a symbol of backwardness and religious extremism and a threat to the values of secularism and women's rights. Another obvious reason was the disappearance of women's traditional fashion with the implementation of neoliberal economic policies, bringing "ready-to wear" affordable, "made in China" scarves, abayas, and jellabas in the local markets. Local manufacture almost died. It should not be forgotten, moreover, that Western wars on Muslim countries and American presence led to an assertion of Muslim identity, especially among young people.

Before the 90s and early 2000s, many women, particularly from the poor classes, either made their owns dresses, or wore traditional garbs: two long pieces of cloth attached at the shoulders with some jewellery or special scarves. They covered their hair, but not necessarily with what we know as a hijab.

Women in urban centres from advantaged socioeconomic back-grounds wore "European" dresses made at home or by local seam-stresses. Other women would still wear casual dresses at home and then cover themselves in *safsari* when going out. Covering a woman's body wasn't always done for religious reasons. Tradition played an impor-tant role, as did modest circumstances in many homes, when there would not be enough time or money to dress up well and do the hair.

Gradually those traditions disappeared, and many women stopped covering their hair with a *safsari*. More and more women dressed à l'européenne. My mother, a seamstress by training and profession, made her owns clothes as well as mine. Few stores with readymade clothes existed back then; most people bought their clothes from sec-ond-hand markets called "friperie" where they arrived in containers from North America or Europe.

It is interesting to note that each time the hijab issue comes up in a public discussion, it is always viewed from a political (secular) and women's-rights angles, but rarely from a fashion point of view or even from an economic perspective. Of course, religion is central in many women's decision to wear the hijab, including myself; however, fashion is a factor for other women and their economic status. The hijab has the further advantage of shielding the wearer from lewd gazes and other forms of harassment. But this doesn't always work.

In Islam, men and women are recommended to dress modestly and treat each other with respect. Many Muslim women believed that if they dressed modestly, they would be immune, whereas if they exposed their skins or their hair, they would be vulnerable. However, in Muslim countries women are harassed regardless. For example, in Egypt there have been calls for the criminalization of street harassment. In 2014, a law was introduced to deter the "harassers." Later new laws stipulated imprisonment and fines. Despite these efforts, sexual harassment still occurs and is even defended by placing the blame on women's dressing and behaviour.

The disappearance of local economies, the loss of traditional skills in weaving, leather treatment, dyeing, and sewing have all added to the emergence of the hijab as a new addition to feminine fashion. The migration of many families from rural villages to big cities for better opportunities compelled many women who still wanted to dress modestly to buy cheap, inexpensive, hijab and long dresses that were available in the souks. Later, the younger generation of women bought tight jeans and tight polyester hijabs from the same souks as well as cheap makeup and skin-lightening products to appear as beautiful as the pop stars they watched on satellite TV from the comfort of their poor neighbourhood homes.

When I arrived in Montreal in 1991, there were few women wearing hijab in the streets. Today, if I go to McGill or the Université de Montréal, the two institutions where I studied, I am sure to see a good number of young women in hijab. But these young people are wearing today a different type of hijab than the one I wore back then. Most of the hijabs today are a long rectangular piece of fabric, like a shawl, and they are wrapped around the head. These kinds of hijab are fashionable and come in different designs. For my first hijab, I bought some monochromatic fabric and asked my mother to make me my own square scarf, which I clipped at the middle of my neck with a safety pin. Today the hijabi young women would also be wearing makeup, this being their way to express their femininity and religious identity. They "belong" to both the sacred and the profane.

Their belonging is also anchored in social media, in Instagram pictures, YouTube clips, in fashionista daily routines, and online tutorials about, for example, how to wrap a crepe georgette nude-tone headscarf. A whole world separates my naïve, simplistic view of thirty years ago with these cosmopolitan, open-minded young women who can be my daughters and who have multiple reasons for wearing hijab: fashion, belonging, identity, and elegance. What makes it easy for them today is the emergence of a whole "modest-fashion" industry. Brands like Zara, H&M, even Dolce & Gabbana are wooing young Muslim millennials by offering them bright coloured headscarves, dress pants, nice long-sleeved shirts, and even long dresses. In the streets of Montreal, in that same province that has made hijab illegal for teachers and public servants, there are stores from local and international brands that cater to this emerging young, educated group of Muslim women born and raised in Canada and proud of their religious identity.

Let's face it. We live in a neoliberal economy that recognizes and believes in one thing: the power of the market. In this economy, we are repeatedly told and constantly reminded through all media that our identities as consumers can bring us closer to happiness. We are defined by the cars we drive, the neighbourhoods we live in, and the brands we wear.

As a Muslim woman who for many years studied economics and finance, I found myself many times trying to answer the following question: what sort of economy do we aspire to? An economic system where we are simply consumers? An economy where the market decides who we are? An economy where "happiness" is a commodity to buy? An economy where our financial worth is the only measure of our achievement? As a Muslim woman, I understand the notion of "dressing" not only as a way to cover my nudity, but most importantly to cover my "vulnerable" sides. I understand clothing as tools or objects to make me feel secure, in a literal as well as a figurative sense.

I see my clothes as agents of protection rather than agents of seduction. What we cover ourselves with is meant to make us look beautiful and confident and protect us from inside and outside. It should bring us closer to each other through mutual awareness, sharing, and compassion and not make us divisive through judgements, competition, and arrogance. The hijab is a spiritual choice in which we renounce the hegemony of the fashion and beauty industries, which impose on us standards that we can never attain.

So how do I feel when I see a Muslim girl appearing on a magazine cover with a beautiful smile and wearing a headscarf, promoting yet another brand? Aren't these corporations simply imposing images of fabricated beauty and success to women? What is even more troubling to me is that this debate about ethical economics is absent in Muslim countries too.

In conclusion, today hijab, beyond its inherently religious meaning, is also a symbol of fashion. Whether we are Muslims or not, whether we agree with the hijab or not, as women we have diverse views about beauty. But for those of us who wear it, the hijab will continue to be part of the equipment that makes us comfortable with our bodies, our mental health, our economic situations, our spirituality.

Hijabi Trends

The hijab had its "golden era" or "peak" during the late 90s. In Muslim countries and in Muslim communities in the West, during these two decades many women started wearing the hijab. Many young Muslim women wore it despite objections from their families. At the time, all hijabs looked similar. The fear that this piece of fabric was instilling among politicians, media, and ignorant individuals was palpable and never understood by me.

In Canada, and for many women of my generation, the hijab became a sort of legacy, a strong religious identity that we wanted to share with the generations following us. For many of us it was a hard-won and rediscovered right, and once in Canada we wanted to raise a generation with the hijab as something natural, where it had a simpler meaning, without any radical religious flavour or political affiliation. It was just a simple extension of a woman's choice in what she wore.

One day some years ago while on a bus in Ottawa I saw to my surprise a group of Somali Muslim teenagers, all wearing the hijab. They were loud and raucous, each with a musical instrument in their hands and a backpack behind them like a turtle shell—the same annoying and nonchalant behaviour as that of other Canadian teenagers. What is ironic is that many of the girls of that same generation, years later as young adult women have decided to take their hijabs off.

Just as there was a wave of women wearing the hijab, there came a new wave of women removing the hijab, or "de-hijabization." But contrary to the panic and fear created by the arrival of the hijab in large numbers, there has been little comment on this latter phenomenon. Besides the obvious fact that the hijab is clearly a choice and a woman can stop wearing it whenever she wishes, there are two other possible reasons for this phenomenon—the institutionalization and banalization of Islamophobia and the influence of social media.

Islamophobia existed before the attacks of 9/11, but after the attacks it was legitimized. Basically, the rhetoric can be summarized as "Muslims attacked us, so it is OK to attack them." Islamophobia arrived in the form of the legal arsenal that came after 9/11, the lining up of legal experts speaking about Islam, air waves filled with stereotypes about Islam, the spreading of misconceptions about Muslims and Muslim women in particular.

For instance, in Quebec the "public debate" around the "reasonable accommodations" marked the first time where it became acceptable to denigrate women wearing hijab. In 2007, in Hérouxville, a small rural community in Central Quebec, the city councillors unanimously adopted a code of conduct for immigrant populations that did not even exist there, prohibiting the stoning or burning of women and requiring them to be taught the importance of Christmas trees. In 2013, the Charter of Values presented by the Parti Québécois government of Pauline Marois, brought this fear of hijabi Muslim women to the centre of the public debate. Everyone had an opinion on the hijab, from Jeanette Bertrand, a popular feminist, to singers like Céline Dion, to writers, politicians, and journalists. People who had probably never met or spoke to a woman wearing a hijab still felt entitled to have an opinion on what these women should wear. It was a sort of public inquisition. The hijab was proclaimed to be a sign of women's oppression and the only way for a Muslim woman to prove that she was not oppressed was to remove her hijab.

In those trying days, I came to know a few women who decided to remove their hijab, expressing fear for their safety and apprehension of public perception. They didn't want to be singled out for their faith. They wanted to blend in. Women in hijab stood out. How many times have I myself felt that significant look from people I come across. Perhaps I imagine it at times, but that only reflects the fear.

In 2008, I was on my way to Canada from a ten-day solidarity trip to Gaza with my Indian Canadian friend. We travelled from Cairo to Paris, where we had to change terminals at the Charles De Gaulle Paris airport to catch our flight to Montreal. A young woman, who ironically was Black, at airport security singled me out for extra inspection. My friend and I had crossed several borders together, including the one between Egypt and Gaza. Never was I stopped or pulled aside more than anyone else. My friend passed through the security line first and she wasn't scanned or body searched. I followed. The border agent stopped me. She was aggressive. She ordered me to open my arms and passed her scanner over my body. My friend was livid. "Why are you stopping my friend? The alarm didn't even beep . . . why?"

The border agent was on a mission. She kept passing her scanner over my body. When she finished, she yelled at us, "Go to your plane . . . go!"

This was one instance of the "public humiliation" that Muslims like me were facing. It is a bit ironic, as I have said, that it was a Black woman, probably originally from a former French colony, who was "doing it" on another racialized woman, born and raised in another former French colony. The woman herself was most likely also a target of racial discrimination, which would explain her extra diligence. She also was being watched. If I were stopped by a white man or woman, I would have felt less disturbed. The colonial dynamics of white against non-white would have been predictable. This incident wasn't the first of its kind and won't be the last. I bring it up to show how some simple acts can become humiliating for a Muslim woman. So why don't we remove our hijab and let life be "normal"?

Given the intensity of the public discourse against the hijab and the backlash women face because of it, the decision to remove the hijab and slip into normal life is therefore understandable.

In recent times there is the social-media fashion aspect of the hijab.

When my daughter was a teenager, she spent many hours watching online videos. "What are you watching?" I would ask, displaying a mother's nosiness. "Dina Tokio" my daughter finally replied one day. And as if to make me feel better, she added that Dina Tokio was a young British Muslim woman YouTuber who give hijab tutorials.

Why would I need to look online for hours to learn how to tie my hijab? All I need is a square piece of fabric, of rayon or light cotton, fold it in two like a triangle, and then put it around my face and use a safety pin to hold the two sides of the triangle together around my face, under my neck. For an occasion, I can go for a silk headscarf and use a nice brooch to cover the safety pin and give a special touch to my outfit.

My daughter didn't agree with my frugal, old-fashioned way to dress. She is a young North American Muslim millennial. She wants to be like her peers. Dina Tokio was their tutor, and on top of that she was cool.

What Dina Tokio did was virtually teach a generation of young Western Muslim girls how to be both fashionable and still modest. This idea seemed to me to be a contradiction. My mother was a seamstress. I grew up with fabrics, dress patterns, fashion magazines all over the places but I was never a fashionista. Even before wearing hijab, fashion was not my strength. My teenage daughter was different. She loved makeup, she loved nice, bright-coloured hijabs, but most of all she found my square hijab terribly out of fashion. Dina Tokio had different ways of wearing her hijab: a tightly tied shawl, a turban, or a simple loose chiffon revealing the earing and part of the neck and some hair at the front.

Dina Torkia is her real name, and she is known to her 800,000 YouTube subscribers as Dina Tokio. She is a British Egyptian Youtuber who was one of the first Muslim women to go online and post daily fashion routines. She became a role model for a whole generation of teenage Muslim girls and young adults. Later, she got married and traveled with her husband in many countries and shared her life with her followers. She was an icon.

But behind the fashion videos there was a new phenomenon emerging: the influencer.

Dina Torkia was an influencer. She was giving hijab tutorials and makeup and fashion advice to her fans. She also became a travel blogger and began giving advice about relationships. Finally, she launched her own fashion line and even published a book called *Modestly*.

For many parents, Dina Tokio had a sort of a reassuring effect: my child is online but in good hands.

However, like any social media phenomenon, there are two sides to the picture. There was the nice, fun, harmless, and cool side: the scarf and beauty tutorials. Behind that there was the dark side: financial profits, a neoliberal model, "exploitation."

Many girls benefited from Dina Tokio. However, they were under the influence of social media in its entirety. By the simple fact of accepting to be users of Facebook, Twitter, or Instagram, we automatically become consumers and our personal information is shared and sold.

In 2019, Dina Torkia announced her decision to stop wearing the hijab "full-time." This is how she explained her decisions to her followers: "The best thing for me personally is not to commit to the hijab daily like I have done for the past twenty years." She added that she "still believes in head-covering as part of her modesty" and that it will "always be a part of her and her heritage, religion, and culture." This decision brought her a huge amount of cyberbullying online. She made a forty-five-minute video about the attacks she received.

We might never know the reasons that pushed this young woman to remove the hijab. It was her personal choice. However, because Dina Torkia isn't a private citizen and wouldn't have been known if she wasn't a Youtuber and an influencer, I think her decision to remove the hijab has undeniably "influenced" many other girls to take the same path and remove their hijabs.

In the late 1990s and early 2000s, Amr Khaled, a teleQuranist from Egypt, convinced thousands of women to wear hijabs. Before even the advent of social media, this preacher-turned-celebrity, without any sophisticated traditional knowledge of Islam, focused on educating people and helping them to "change their lives." Wearing a hijab, to be good to your elderly parents, to be a good citizen—Amr Khaled spoke on such matters to millions of his followers on Satellite TV. Many women liked his simple message. I asked a cousin in Tunisia, the only member in her family to start wearing the hijab, why she decided to wear it. "Amr Khaled" she candidly replied. "I wanted to be a good Muslim and he had the words to convince me."

Thus, wearing the hijab or removing it is influenced by surrounding fashion trends. No one is immune. To keep framing hijab as a misogynist symbol or as an oppressive tool is overlooking all the complexities around it; it is an attempt to infantilize women either through patronizing them or through reducing their decisions to *one* simplistic reason.

Islam and Feminism

In 2009, in Kuala Lumpur, Zainah Anwar and other Muslim women founded an organization called Musawah. In Arabic, *Musawah* means "equality." Its founders described it as a "global movement for equality and justice in the Muslim Family."

In the 1980s, another NGO, Sisters in Islam, also established in Malaysia, had already started its advocacy work for Muslim women's rights and discriminatory family laws. The main objective of these organizations is to provide Muslim women with a third option. For centuries, stuck between two polarizing views, secular liberation (imported from the West) and Islamic oppression (inherited from old patriarchal norms), Muslim women were now organizing themselves and finding their liberation in the same religious texts that once were used to discriminate against them. Islamic Feminism was born.

In her description of Islamic Feminism, Ziba Mir-Hosseini, one of the founders of Musawah, writes:

> Faced by an apparent choice between the devil of those who want to impose patriarchal interpretations of Islam's sacred texts, and the deep blue sea of those who pursue a neo-colonialist hegemonic global project in the name of enlightenment and feminism, those of us committed to achieving justice for women and a just world have no other option than to bring Islamic and feminist

perspectives together. Otherwise, Muslim women's quest for equality will remain hostage to different political forces and tendencies, as it was in the twentieth century and continues to be in the new century that began with the war on terror.[1]

Islamic Feminism is not a disguised "tool of neocolonialism" or another brown version of white feminism; it fills a void created by centuries of inaction and women's deprivation of justice under the name of religion. The first major research project Musawah took on was a study of the common ground between the UN Convention on the Elimination of All Forms of Discrimination against Women (CEDAW) and Muslim family laws. In 2020, Musawah launched a campaign bringing together advocates for family law reform from three regions—the Middle East and North Africa, Sub-Saharan Africa, and South and Southeast Asia—for issues like consent to marriage, divorce rights, polygamy, and inheritance rights. In her book *Do Muslim Women Need Saving?* Lila Abu-Lughod, without demeaning the efforts of these organizations to improve the lives of Muslim women, finds limits to their efforts. These are the same limits that face the work of secular women's rights groups.

She says, "We need to be attentive to the intersection of rights work with a range of global and class inequalities." She adds, "The intellectual tools of the rights frames (Islamic Feminism) that are common sense now turn out to be inextricable from the socially located political projects of the people and groups who put them to use. They are also not adequate for appreciating the complexities of women's experience." According to Abu-Lughod, Muslim women go through a "matrix of oppression," which includes the political, the economic, and the mundane varieties. From her study of the lives of Egyptian Bedouin women, Abu-Lughod draws surprising examples of how Muslim women have found their liberation through their religion. Many of these women, despite their oppressive conditions, have no choice but to stay in them because of police abuse, political corruption, and economic policies that keep them poor. If we want to "save" Muslim women, we need to "save" them from the lack of opportunities dictated by their conditions.

Within this matrix of oppression, Islamic values and traditions can sometimes be a liberating force.

Applying these arguments to my case, I grew up in a country where it wasn't easy to be a woman. There was male privilege, domestic abuse, and sexual harassment. Many times, I envied male privilege. A boy always wins even when he is the loser. Nevertheless, I never felt that this male privilege was given to men by Islam. To the contrary, I found my empowerment and strength in the Quran and my spirituality. Practicing Islam appeased my perpetual quest for answers. This is what kept me and keeps me going. Is religion my "opiate," then? I don't believe so. Religion for me is not an escape from reality, as "opium" would suggest. My belief gives a spiritual sense to my battles. My wins and my losses will always have meanings. It gives me a holistic understanding of the world.

Coming to Canada, I thought at first that women's rights were better here. During my interview to obtain the *Certificat de sélection* (immigration papers), the Quebec representative at the Canadian embassy said to me in a patronizing voice, "In Quebec, women go to coffee shops!" I didn't care. I went to coffee shops in Tunis with my dad when I was a young girl, and I didn't like them because of the smoke and the noise.

Cafés were places where men socialized, smoked, drank, and stared at passersby, especially women. In poor and populous neighbourhoods, and in some downtown areas, they are male territories, where unemployed men, young, adults, and seniors would fill their days talking politics and soccer, playing cards, smoking cigarettes or shisha, sipping coffee, tea, lemonade, watching soccer games, or simply staring some more.

In upscale neighbourhoods, cafés were destinations for couples, young people, and families. They weren't the monopoly of men. I went to several of these places with my male and female friends. They never made me feel liberated.

It didn't occur to me that going to a café was a sign of women's liberation. Obviously, the French Canadian woman at the interview was projecting her own beliefs or her own understanding of feminism on me, the Muslim Arab girl, who was interested in higher ideals, in higher goals: to live my spirituality as I wanted, to be able to study finance, to write op-eds in newspapers, to speak politics freely. I wish she had asked me about my own aspirations and how Canada would help me achieve them. Why do I always have to be judged through the eyes of others?

When I first landed in Montreal, indeed I saw girls going to bars like men, and I found that women had access to better education and health. But I was also startled by other things. I found that violence against women was widespread. Women disappeared. Just like in Tunisia, most women were paid less than men, and many low-paid jobs were reserved for women. I found that women struggled to get access to abortion clinics. I found that women were poorly represented at the boards of companies, in political parties, in higher positions.

Today, after the #metoo movement, to my immense surprise, I discovered that what was happening in many so-called traditional societies, in terms of sexual harassment and sexual abuse, was also rampant in the so-called modern societies.

The praxis of oppression is similar between these two societies, Tunisia and Quebec. Wealth may hide it, very well sometimes, but it doesn't make it disappear. As a little girl growing up in one of those so-called traditional societies, I was made to believe, mainly through French books, movies, newspapers, and magazines, that our fate as women was a direct result of our religion: Islam. And in that regard, if we wanted to be "liberated," "free," and "enlightened," we Muslim Arab girls had to abandon Islam. But I didn't run away from my religion; instead, I found solace in it. I found many answers, I found my strength.

Privilege and Solidarity

Years ago, after reading *Lean In* by Sheryl Sandberg, I couldn't stop comparing myself to her. Sheryl Sandberg is my age. We grew up in a middle-class family and went to business school. But the similarities ended there.

Sheryl Sandberg became one of the most powerful and successful women in the US. In her rise professionally, she had powerful mentors like Larry Summers, Secretary of the Treasury under the Clinton administration. And so, despite the fact that our paths seem to have been quite similar, at least from the beginning until we finished university, there are plenty of differences. In Tunisia I never had a mentor. Nobody believed in me, except my parents. No Tunisian Larry Summers hired me or pushed me forward to succeed. To the contrary, I was implicitly pushed aside because I didn't conform to mainstream society's moulds. The Tunisian government of the time did all it could to strip me of my rights to a scholarship because I was wearing the hijab. I was considered a fundamentalist. My success as a female student wearing a headscarf wasn't something to be proud of. Only "liberated" women could be successful. Only women who conformed to the politics of that government were celebrated as successful. The minute you showed dissent, political or religious, you were erased from the mainstream picture of success. You didn't belong to the elite; you were not presented as a role model for the youth. You ceased to exist.

When I came to Canada I was given—I thought—a second chance, a new opportunity to build a new life and develop my true self. As a new immigrant I realized I had not only to be good but exceptional in order to be noticed. I never was in a position to have the luxury to lean back. I always looked forward, climbed ladder after ladder, only to find closed doors and sent back to start again. I understood that no matter how far and how hard you leaned, when you are starting from below the bottom you will never reach the summits of the world in which Sheryl Sandberg lives.

As an immigrant Arab Muslim woman, I was starting very low. In Canada, I had mentors, one of whom was my thesis director at McGill University. He believed in me and defended me when others put obstacles before me. But he wasn't trying to find me a job at the Bank of Canada or in the Department of Finance; he was trying to keep me in a university program. My feminism is one of survival, not of ambition. For many other minority women, this is a known story.

Later, Alexa McDonough, former leader of the New Democratic Party of Canada, stood beside me and my children when the Government of Canada let my husband down. Once again, I wasn't fighting to become successful in the world of politics or business; I was fighting for my rights to be treated with dignity and justice. I was fighting for the bare minimum.

In contrast to Sheryl Sandberg, I didn't have a nanny to take care of my kids when I went out to defend my husband's rights. I didn't have a partner, because he was illegally in jail for over a year and being tortured. I had my mother who stood beside me all the way.

My road is not unique. There are many other women in Canada and elsewhere who "lean in" every day as single mothers, as First Nations people, immigrants, refugees, and underprivileged members of society. They are not fighting to sit at the same tables as privileged male CEOs, their battles are to get a job, to feed their families, to protect themselves from harassment. Their battles aren't always recognized, most of the times they are dismissed. But the stories of their struggles are as important, if not more.

A few years ago I met a famous author. She had made her position in the world and I had looked up to her. We had a positive conversation about women's rights. She asked me about women's rights in Tunisia.

Apparently she had heard great things about the feminist movement in that country. I told her bluntly that if it wasn't for the poor Tunisian women working to the bone as maids in the cities, cleaning for them, the committed and praised Tunisian feminists wouldn't be around today.

I was taken back when my interlocutor quickly shot back that if it wasn't for the maids, we wouldn't have the great work of Virginia Woolf. I replied that first of all not all the women who hired maids were the likes of Virginia Woolf and that this argument wouldn't make the treatment and hiring of maids more ethical. I could have asked, Who was Virginia Woolf to the Tunisians? She is a heroine of the Western world.

In her book, *Mrs Woolf and the Servants*, British scholar Alison Light painted a pained relationship between employer and domestic worker, shedding a light on a society that was structured around class, where the "terrible mental and emotional distress" of the maids were dismissed, including by Virginia Woolf. "I am an individual," Agnes Smith, one of Woolf's domestics reproached her, "as unique in my way as you are in yours."

When I was growing up in Tunisia, my father refused adamantly to have a maid in our home. His arguments were mainly privacy, financial and, frankly, patriarchal. My mother and I had a different position. My mother worked full time and I was in high school and soon to join university. My mother split the housework fairly between me and my brother. After he left for his studies, I found myself with most of the cleaning. My mom cooked for us. On Sundays my mother washed our clothes. My father did the groceries, paid the bills, and took care of the garden but didn't do any cleaning at home. My mother kept her income for herself. My father never made her pay any bill. He even borrowed money from her when he was financially squeezed, and he would reimburse her later. It wasn't the perfect situation. My father never liked the fact that my mother worked outside the home, but my mother had both financial independence and a thriving social life.

After complaining to my mother that I had exams to prepare for and that I couldn't always clean the house, she decided to hire a maid once per week to clean the floors, scrub the bathroom and the toilet. My father was not happy, but my mother paid for the service. We kept that maid for a few months. My father kept nagging, and my mother finally decided to let her go. I kept cleaning the house on the weekends. All my friends had maids, their mothers and fathers working outside the homes. I was different.

On one hand, I badly wanted the help, on the other, I felt somehow "empowered" by cleaning the house. Moreover, my political and religious conscience had started to steer me away from "hiring" other people to serve me, especially for demeaning tasks. I didn't want to have people work for me because I believe I can never be fair to them. The power relations are so obvious: class and money. Through the years, I became more efficient at cleaning; I found it exhausting. Nevertheless, I couldn't accept myself sitting down relaxing while another woman, weaker than me, cleaning my bathroom dirt. First, I have cleaning standards that I was convinced the maid wouldn't always meet. Moreover, I would expect to be annoyed with her, hurting her feelings, blaming her for not cleaned enough or properly. Lastly, I would feel ashamed that someone else was cleaning after me.

Sharing with me some of her impressions about spending her summer in Tunisia, a cousin of mine living in Italy recently told me that the normal lives of many privileged Tunisian households would just freeze if the maid didn't show up for a day. "I will cut her salary!" "She is so lazy, that bitch!" I was horrified but not surprised. I had grown up hearing and seeing exactly the same attitudes, but hoped that with time, they would disappear. They didn't.

We can't continue to accept the myth of Tunisian or any other feminism if the "domestic helpers" are not recognized as the helpers and supporters of the "educated" women who use their services. Until the rights of these maids are protected and enforced by law, such feminism will be incomplete.

The Evolving Hijab

When I was a girl, we used to live near a large public park. Central Park *à la tunisienne*. It is called the "Le Belvédère" and is an island of greenery in the heart of a city threatened by sprawling urbanism and desertification. It had a zoo and a playground for children. Playgrounds were not common in my childhood. Going there was like heaven. Near the playground, there was a carousel and some rides: a paradise for the girl I was. My favourite ride was a rocket spaceship because it made me feel like I was traveling in the sky among planets and stars. I closed my eyes and let my imagination run wild as the heavy rocket filled with screaming kids went upwards, suddenly touched the shaky wooden platform, and soared once more in the opposite direction. I didn't want the ride to stop. I kept asking my dad for another ride, then another one, and another one, until he ran out patience and money.

Then suddenly I was a teenager and I stopped going to the rides, but my love of challenges and risks didn't cease. A few weeks before writing my Baccalauréat exam, a national high school competition to enter university, I decided with some of my friends to go to the rides: it was our way to decompress. All types of rides were there: the mighty roller coaster, the classic carousel, but this time my favourite was the Rotor, what we called the "Sieve" in our Tunisian dialect. We saw our friends who had not joined us look like pixelated pictures before they suddenly disappeared in a black swoosh as the Rotor took speed and my mind whirled: Greek mathematical symbols colliding with DNA sequences memorized from my biology lessons slowly disintegrating at Bachelard's *epistemological break*. The "Sieve," whose mechanics was based on the centrifugal force, would dissipate my worries, unclog my brain cells, and I felt lighter and cleaner and ready to confront one of the first and cruellest exams of adulthood.

A fundamental principle in finance is that the higher the risk, the higher the rate of return. I applied it to my career. After I obtained a tenure-track position at a Canadian university, I decided to resign. It was a risk to drop my academic career to start another one in writing. Was the rate of return high? Financially, it wasn't. Most writers know how difficult it is to sell books and establish a strong and committed readership.

Where do amusement park rides factor into all of this? The last time I went on one was the Behemoth at Canada's Wonderland. A few seconds after I jumped enthusiastically into the seat with my teenage kids, I dreaded it. I was scared. It seems that with age, I had developed what in finance we call *risk aversion*. When my feet touched the ground again, I swore to myself that I wouldn't take any rides anymore!

About thirty years ago, I decided to put on the hijab. It was one of the most difficult decisions in my adult life. From the camp of the "modern" I switched to the camp of the "backward." From the group of the "normal," I jumped to the "abnormal," I became a social embarrassment for some, an extremist, a "khowanjia" (a member of the Muslim Brotherhood), or a "khomeynist" (a supporter of Imam Khomeini and by extension of the Islamic Iranian Revolution). Wearing a hijab became my new identity, whether I liked it or not.

I always remember myself as a spiritual person, going to the mosque with my father, reading the Quran, reading histories of Islam, the prophets, other religions. My environment was not particularly religious. I would say my relatives and friends were cultural Muslims, not very observant. At school, the worst subject for us was "Civic and Islamic education." The professor usually lacked the passion, the knowledge, and the pedagogical tools for it. Everybody waited for the teacher to finish his or her rant and most of the students cheated on exams by writing little notes to memorize the verses or Hadith. Tunisia was cracking down on the Islamists. Immediately after deciding to wear the hijab, I became considered by the authorities as an Islamist. The hijab was the "banner of political Islam" as they put it. I became that banner. This is all to say that my "Islamic identity" wasn't forged in school. My family wasn't also particularly religious. We were practicing but not deeply conservative. My father never asked me to cover my hair. He wasn't very happy when I told him that I was going to start wearing the hijab, but he reluctantly accepted my decision.

Wearing a hijab was for me and will always be a deeply religious act. Before wearing a hijab, I had a double life. From what I was wearing and how I looked, nobody would have thought that I was religious or that I would go home and pray. Being one person at home and leaving all this behind me to become another person outside and show that I fitted into "modern society," that I was a liberated girl who could do whatever she wished, didn't make me feel at peace with myself. I call it the Schizophrenic Identity Syndrome. Outside, like all the teenage girls of my age, I was asked to be interested in fashion, make-up, boys. Then came my moment of introspection, and I realized that I was not really interested and not ready to embrace all those things. They didn't fit my personality and they didn't fit my spiritual being. Nevertheless, social pressure, peer pressure, culture, tradition, everyone around me pulled me towards the norm.

Be normal, I kept being told. But what is being normal? I questioned the cultural expectations about the role of women, I questioned the cultural expectations about how we were supposed to dress and please boys and men. Why did I have to do my eyebrows, or straighten my hair, or be thin? Why did I have to enhance my breasts in a nice tight dress or shirt? Islam, as I understood it, allowed me to be myself and to be accountable to God only and not to society or the surrounding culture. For some, Islam is an oppression, for me it is liberation. And indeed, I felt a sense of relief after starting to wear the hijab. A relief from those boxes waiting for me to be fitted in them.

With that sense of relief came the strength to defend my choice. I was always asked, put on the defensive, if not attacked by question after question about the reasons that pushed me to wear the hijab. No matter how well I answered and how sophisticated or how simplistic my answers were, they were rarely met with conviction or satisfaction.

There must be a brother hidden behind my back forcing me to cover, or a despotic father brainwashing me, or an abusive mother, trying to make me look like her, or a sheikh whispering in my ears. My choice was never accepted as it was: a mature, considered decision with a strong desire to follow my Islamic faith and teachings.

Much has changed. I am older, I live in Canada, and the hijab has gone through many trials and political battles. With time also, the meaning of the hijab has evolved. Yes, it is still about modesty, but for me it is also an identity symbol and a sign of resistance to all other society "norms." Not necessarily sexual expectations, but consumerism, a woman's self-consciousness of her age, body shape, and beauty, the pressure of a fashion establishment that targets girls and women of all ages. In other words, the new boxes prepared for me when I was twenty by an Arab, secular society with an Islamic flavour were replaced thirty year later by other prettier boxes but still as hollow and superficial as the former: middle-aged women should dye their hair, should be physically fit and wear body-fitting clothes and perhaps go for plastic surgery to look younger and get closer to the beauty standards set by the fashion industry. I didn't want to fit into these boxes and my hijab came to symbolize this resistance.

Ironically, I look around me and many of the young and older women wearing a hijab today are not bothered by these new boxes. Even if the hijab was for years wrongly described as a sign of women's oppression, some smart businesses have today embraced it, not for ideological reasons but for profit. "If life gives you lemons, make lemonade" seems to be the motto. Hijab, once a lemon, became a lucrative lemonade opportunity for many businesses. Muslim YouTube influencers teach young hijabi fashionistas how to wrap their hijabs ("Hijabi [Wrap My Hijab]" is even the title of a famous hip-hop song by an American Muslim singer, Mona Haydar), and how to make their heads look bigger in a hijab (*Does My Head Look Big in This* is the title of a book for teenagers written by an Australian Muslim author), how to put makeup to highlight your eyes. In a nutshell, how to be a modern *hijabi* (a word used to name women who wear the hijab). The hijab became a brand, and *hijabis*, those who wear it, potential customers, a market to be conquered.

Gone are my naïve ideals of resistance, of social justice, of equality, that accompanied my deeply religious journey with the hijab. Gone are those ideals, taken away by a globalized world, where even modesty became a commodity traded by powerful multinational corporations.

Obviously, symbols evolve and even lose their original meaning and intent. What is radical at one time becomes accepted later and can acquire new meaning. The hijab, though a statement of resistance or fashion, is still often perceived by the unsophisticated as a sign of oppression thus putting the lives of Muslim women in danger from hate groups.

Conclusion

Hijab was and will remain a complex symbol. Some will see it as a sign of oppression and others will find in it the confidence they look for and a sense of identity. Others will see it as a symbol of liberation. When I wore a hijab, I thought all my problems would be solved. They were just beginning. Tunisia, the country where I was born and raised, tried for years to ban it from high schools, universities, and workplaces. The arguments for that ban were political: stop extremism and defeat the Islamists. I never belonged to any Islamic party. Nevertheless, I was branded an extremist or a terrorist just because I decided to wear a headscarf to respect a religious recommendation I deeply understood as part of my faith.

Today, hijab in Tunisia is visible everywhere in the public space. Women are relatively free to wear what they wish. The emerging democracy that is being built since the Arab Spring in 2011 opened the door to some positive changes. Women are not left to choose between their faith and their jobs. They can have both. However, that doesn't mean that patriarchy disappeared, or women's rights are written in stone. Things are still fragile.

When I arrived in Canada, hijab was very rare. The 9/11 attacks, the antiterrorism legislation that ensued, later the debate about "reasonable accommodation" in Quebec, followed by the failed attempt of Quebec's Charter of Values, the other failed attempt by Prime Minister Stephen Harper's government to ban the niqab at Citizenship ceremonies and its attempts to vilify Islamic dressing, and more recently the passing of a legislation in Quebec that bans the wearing of religious symbols by teachers, police officers, judges, and other public servants created a stuffed atmosphere where hate towards Muslim women wearing hijab became almost routine. Prior to these events, Islamophobia existed. These events made it normal. Many women across Canada were attacked.

Islamophobia towards women isn't only about a woman being physically or verbally abused in the street; it is also always about a job denied, or a stare in the bus, or forms of microaggressions. Islamophobia is a form of racism that is embedded in many of our institutions and in many minds. It is found at both institutional and personal levels. To combat this phenomenon, we need to acknowledge it first. Its existence is often denied, and instead Muslims are urged to "integrate," build a thicker skin and accept criticism.

In 2021, in the aftermath of the hate crime that killed a family of Canadian Muslims and left their nine-year-old son orphaned, the Canadian government held a summit on Islamophobia. I sat in front of my computer for about six hours watching activists, politicians, academics explicate the phenomenon. I watched with a feeling of déjà-vu. Yes, I knew the sad statistics, I knew the feelings of fear, I knew about the surveillance programs that target mosques and infiltrate Muslim communities. Many things were shared but many others remained to be told.

The purpose behind this book is not to garner pity as a victim or lament my fate. I want to draw attention to the fact that our laws, our media, our politicians, and our institutions have contributed to this phenomenon. I've always wanted to add my voice to the calls for justice. Canada was founded on a land that was colonized. Over the decades its indigenous population was robbed, caricatured, demeaned, and brutalized. Thousands of women and men from the First Nations were killed, their cultures erased, and their children sent to schools where they suffered from physical and sexual abuse, and were forced to reject their native ways and languages.

Compared to theirs, my suffering is benign. Maybe I should shut up. Compared to that of Black Canadians my ordeal might be seen as a simple poke in the face. But in human suffering there isn't a scale. There is not one accepted injustice and another that should be denounced.

"Injustice anywhere is a threat to justice everywhere."

Today, we are at a crossroads. The Canadian government has finally acknowledged that there is a problem called Islamophobia and that Muslim women are easy targets for attacks. In this book I have argued that Islamophobia has deep roots in the anti-terrorism legislations, in laws passed to target religious symbols like hijab, in the media's continual stereotypical portrayals of Muslim women and men, in imperialist wars and military occupations of Muslim countries. Change will be slow and difficult. But it must happen, and we should continue to fight for it.

I hope that through this book my readers will understand my decision to wear the hijab and the struggle I went through. Every woman has a story, and each story is worth listening to. Many times, I thought of putting a premature end to this book. It was emotionally draining, and a nagging internal voice kept questioning me about its relevancy. I refused to pose as a victim, and I knew I couldn't speak on behalf of all Muslim women. I didn't want to fall into the generalization trap or make easy judgement of other women's choices.

I presented my manuscript to several Canadian publishers, in the belief that they would be excited by it. At a time of increasing recognition of the nation's diversity, it seemed that a memoir such as mine would be the perfect vehicle to "educate" readers about Muslim women and the hijab, which has been so misunderstood and raised such controversy. Unfortunately, I got either refused or simply ignored by most of the mainstream (ie large) publishers. Accompanied by patronizing words, their response, when it came, was simply that this wouldn't be a subject of much interest to readers and the book wouldn't sell. I was left with the impression that my story didn't matter. I understood from their reaction that the majority of Canadians have no interest in Islam and the plight of hijabi Muslim women. When Mawenzi House expressed interest in the manuscript, I felt greatly relieved and happy. But beyond my selfish enthusiasm, the decision of Mawenzi to publish my work is a bittersweet message. Yes, my work will be finally available to Canadians, but it took a publisher that specializes in "diaspora" stories to see the importance and relevance of my work.

Every October is Islamic History Month. It was in 2007 that the House of Commons adopted a motion, an initiative led by the late Member of Parliament Mauril Bélanger, to give the tenth month of the calendar such a designation. Unfortunately, few Canadians are aware of it, though every year several Canadian Muslim organizations celebrate it among themselves together with a few "usual suspect" allies, with movie and food festivals and conferences.

Islamophobia and the plight of Muslim women isn't an issue that Canadian Muslims should carry alone on their shoulders. The same thing can be said about all forms of racism, of course. They are the business of *all* Canadians.

Many times, I have witnessed the power of people coming together to fight injustice. While my husband was detained abroad, and while I canvassed as a political candidate, and while I worked as a human rights activist, fighting antiterrorism measures and advocating for civil rights, I met with people of all faiths, political views, sexual orientations, and ethnic backgrounds. I was then able to regain my faith in humanity. So why don't we look beyond hijab and learn to understand each other?

Acknowledgements

Writing a book is never an easy task. But bringing our own vulnerabilities adds another level of difficulty. I am very grateful to the persistent support of many of my friends: Fred. A. Reed, Caroline Lavoie, Tara Collins, Pamela Walker, and many others. Our long conversations, their encouragement, and even criticisms are so valuable. I am thankful to the financial support of the Canada Council for the Arts.

A special thanks to my colleagues at Carleton University, Department of English Language and Literature, professors Nadia Bozak, Dana Dragunoiu and Janice Shroeder, for inviting me to speak and read some excerpts of this book while still in the making.

Warm thanks go to the Mawenzi team for the comments, edits, and support. I am very grateful for the confidence and trust Nurjehan Aziz showed me.

Last my not least, my family has been a solid rock holding my back. My mother, my children, Barâa and Houd and my partner Maher. I wouldn't have been able to finish this work without their love.

References

Introduction: Why English

1. Marilyn Hacker, "I Write in French to Tell the French I Am Not French," *Words Without Borders*, January 1, 2019, https://wordswithoutborders.org/read/article/2019-01/january-2019-i-write-in-french-to-tell-the-french-i-am-not-marilyn-hacker/.

An Urgent Calling

1. Angus Reid Institute, "Islamophobia in Canada: Four mindsets indicate negativity is nationwide, most intense in Quebec," March 13, 2023, https://angusreid.org/islamophobia-canada-quebec/.

Growing Up As a Muslim Woman in Tunisia

1. "Interview with Naama the Lady of Tunisian Song," August 15, 2013, https://www.youtube.com/watch?v=zj84cs9YTDU.

The Innocent Islamophobia

1. Homa Hoodfar, "The Veil in Their Minds and on Our Heads: Veiling Practices and Muslim Women," in *Women, Gender and Religion: A Reader*, edited by Elizabeth A Castelli, 420-446, (New York: Palgrave, 2001).

Hijab and Public Transit

1. Ryan Tumilty, "OC Transpo driver who confronted Islamophobia succumbs to cancer," *CBC News*, August 22, 2018, https://www.cbc.ca/news/canada/ottawa/alain-charette-dies-cancer-1.4795269.

Hijab and the Media

1. Sut Jhally, "Edward Said: on 'Orientalism,'" Media Education Foundation, Challenging Media, released in 2005. https://www.mediaed.org/transcripts/Edward-Said-On-Orientalism-Transcript.pdf.

2. Mariam Khan, "Muslims are still misrepresented in film and TV, so how do we change the script," *Stylist*, 2021, https://www.stylist.co.uk/entertainment/muslim-representation-film-tv/543599

3. Peter Zimonjic, "Trudeau says Bloc leader is using 'coded' language in attack on Transport Minister Omar Alghabra," *CBC News*, January 15, 2021, https://www.cbc.ca/news/politics/omar-alghabra-minister-bloc-blanchet-trudeau-1.5875222.

4. Emily Stewart, "Watch John McCain defend Barack Obama against a racist voter in 2008," *Vox*, Updated September 1, 2018, https://www.vox.com/policy-and-politics/2018/8/25/17782572/john-mccain-barack-obama-statement-2008-video.

Hijab and Politics

1. Paul Journet, "Charte: Bernard Drainville s'attaque à 'un malaise,'" *La Presse*, September, 11, 2013, https://www.lapresse.ca/actualites/politique/politique-quebecoise/201309/10/01-4688061-charte-bernard-drainville-sattaque-a-un-malaise.php.

2. Katia Gagnon, "Les femmes voilées sont 'manipulées' dit Jeanette Bertrand," *La Presse*, October 16, 2013, https://plus.lapresse.ca/screens/48c9-460c-525d604d-bc14-13e7ac1c6068%7C_0.html.

3. Laura Payton, "For campaign magic, Harper turns to a wizard from Oz," *Macleans*, September 10, 2015, https://macleans.ca/politics/ottawa/for-campaign-magic-harper-turns-to-a-wizard-from-oz/.

4. Anne Kingston, "Why Stephen Harper doesn't want to talk about 'women's issues,'" *Macleans*, September 11, 2015, https://www.macleans.ca/politics/ottawa/why-stephen-harper-doesnt-want-to-talk-about-womens-issues/.

Gendered Islamophobia in Numbers

1. Joanna Slater and Niha Masih, "As the world looks for coronavirus scapegoats, Muslims are blamed in India," *The Washington Post*, April 23, 2020.

2. Imran Awan, "Debunking five social media myths about Muslims and coronavirus," *Middle East Eye*, April 23, 2020, https://www.middleeasteye.net/opinion/coronavirus-muslims-britain-five-social-media-myths.

3. Andrea Huncar, "Far-right extremists getting bolder as threatening behaviour goes unchecked, police warned," *CBC News Edmonton*, May 11, 2020, https://www.cbc.ca/news/canada/edmonton/ramadan-bombathon-edmonton-mosque-far-right-extremists-police-charges-1.5564323.

4. "Hijab-wearing woman attacked in Metro urges others to don religious symbols," *CBC News*, January 13, 2014, https://www.cbc.ca/news/canada/montreal/hijab-wearing-woman-attacked-in-metro-urges-others-to-don-religious-symbols-1.2494575.

5. Ethan Cox, "More Islamophobia in Quebec," *National Post*, February 3, 2014, https://nationalpost.com/opinion/ethan-cox-more-islamophobia-in-quebec.

6. Ali Raza, "Anti-Muslim hate 'normalized' for too long, say many in Muslim community mourning deadly London attack," *CBC News Toronto*, June 8, 2021, https://www.cbc.ca/news/canada/toronto/london-attack-islamophobia-1.6058161.

7. Steve Rukavina, "New research shows Bill 21 having 'devastating' impact on religious minorities in Quebec," *CBC News*, August 4, 2022, https://www.cbc.ca/news/canada/montreal/bill-21-impact-religious-minorities-survey-1.6541241.

The Multiple Layers of Hate

1. Rania Rizvi, "Internalized Islamophobia: 9/11's insidious aftermath," *The Daily Targum*, Cornell University, December 9, 2020, https://dailytargum.com/article/2020/12/internalized-islamophobia-9-11s-insidious-aftermath.

2. Kim Berry, "The symbolic use of Afghan women in the war on terror," *Humboldt Journal of Social Relations*, Vol 27, no 2 (2003): 137-160.

3. "George Bush says Afghan girls will suffer 'unspeakable harm' after US withdrawal," *The National News*, July 14, 2021, https://www.thenationalnews.com/world/us-news/2021/07/14/george-bush-says-afghan-girls-will-suffer-unspeakable-harm-after-us-withdrawal/.

4. "Afghan Activist: George W Bush's Claim US War in Afghanistan Protected Women Is a 'Shameless Lie,'" *Democracy Now*, Jul 15 2021, https://www.democracynow.org/2021/7/15/afghanistan_taliban_us_withdrawal.

Systemic Islamophobia or a Few Bad Apples?

1. "Canada, Parliament, House of Commons, "M-103 Systemic Racism and religious discrimination., 42nd Parliament, 1st Session, March 23, 2017, https://www.ourcommons.ca/members/en/88849/motions/8661986.

2. "Man charged in stabbing death of Etobicoke mosque caretaker," *CBC News*, September 18, 2020, https://www.cbc.ca/news/canada/toronto/man-charged-death-mosque-caretaker-1.5730329.

3. Barbara Perry and Ryan Scrivens, "Uneasy Alliances: A Look at the Right-Wing Extremist Movement in Canada," *Studies in Conflict & Terrorism*, Vol 39, no 9, (2016): 819-841, September 15, 2015.

4. "Quebec doesn't have a problem with Islamophobia, Premier Legault says," *CBC News*, January 31, 2019, https://www.cbc.ca/news/canada/montreal/quebec-mosque-shooting-islamophobia-1.5000950.

5. Paula McCooey, "Federal funding helps increase security at Muslim places of worship," *The Ottawa Citizen*, November 27, 2017, https://ottawacitizen.com/news/local-news/federal-funding-helps-to-protect-muslim-community.

6. Steve Arnold, "Hamilton rabbis express horror at killing of Muslim family in London," *The Hamilton Jewish News*, June 11, 2021, https://www.hamiltonjewishnews.com/news/hamilton-rabbis-express-horror-at-killing-of-muslim-family-in-london.

Colonialism and Women

1. Josh Crabb, "Canadians need to understand impacts of colonization, MMIWG advocate says," *CTV News Winnipeg*, September 29, 2021, https://winnipeg.ctvnews.ca/canadians-need-to-understand-impacts-of-colonization-mmiwg-advocate-says-1.5605936.

2. "Colonising Algeria was crime against humanity, Macron," *The Morning Call, Africa News*, February 17, 2017, https://www.youtube.com/watch?v=nvV43ICfMWE.

3. "France's Macron: No Repentance Nor Apologies for Algeria Occupation During Independence War," *VOA News*, January 20, 2021, https://www.voanews.com/a/europe_frances-macron-no-repentance-nor-apologies-algeria-occupation-during-independence-war/6200981.html.

4. Mark Kennedy, "'Simply a savage': How the residential schools came to be," *The Ottawa Citizen*, May 22, 2015, https://ottawacitizen.com/news/politics/simply-a-savage-how-the-residential-schools-came-to-be.

5. Earl of Cromer, *Modern Egypt*, 2 vols (New York: Macmillan, 1908).

6. Malika Rahal, "Algeria: Nonviolent resistance against French colonialism, 1830s-1950s," edited by Maciej J Bartkowski, Rienner, pp.107-223, 2013, ffhal-01316088.

Islam and Feminism

1. Ziba Mir-Hosseini, "Beyond 'Islam' vs 'Feminism,'" *Institute of Development Studies*, Vol 42, no 1, (January 2011). https://images.shulcloud.com/14262/uploads/Jeannettes-Class-Documents/WeekThree/BeyondIslamvsFeminism.pdf:

Bibliography

Introduction: Why English

Hacker, Marilyn. "I Write in French to Tell the French I Am Not French." *Words Without Borders*. January 1, 2019. https://wordswithoutborders.org/read/article/2019-01/january-2019-i-write-in-french-to-tell-the-french-i-am-not-marilyn-hacker/

Quinn, Ben. "French police make woman remove clothing on Nice beach following burkini ban." *The Guardian*. August 24, 2016. https://www.theguardian.com/world/2016/aug/24/french-police-make-woman-remove-burkini-on-nice-beach.

Scott, Joan Wallach. *The Politics of the Veil*. Princeton: Princeton University Press, 2007.

An Urgent Calling

Angus Reid Institute. "Islamophobia in Canada: Four mindsets indicate negativity is nationwide, most intense in Quebec." March 13, 2023. https://angusreid.org/islamophobia-canada-quebec/

What Is Islamophobia

Dinet, Étienne and Sliman Ben Brahim. *L'Orient vu de l'Occident*. Paris: Édition Héritage, 2021.

Islamophobia Research & Documentation Project. "Defining 'Islamophobia.'" *Center for Race & Gender*, University of California at Berkeley. 2013. https://web.archive.org/web/20170309201925/http://crg.berkeley.edu/content/islamophobia/defining-islamophobia

Kanji, Azeezah, et al. "Islamophobia in Canada." Report submitted to Standing Committee on Canadian Heritage on November 10, 2017. https://noorculturalcentre.ca/wp-content/uploads/2018/01/Islamophobia-in-Canada-2017.pdf

Karaoglu, Seyda Nur. "A Definition of Islamophobia in Étienne Dinet's The Pilgrimage to the Sacred House of Allah." Master's thesis, George Washington University, 2018.

The Runnymede Trust Report. "Islamophobia: A Challenge for Us All." 1997. https://www.runnymedetrust.org/publications/islamophobia-a-challenge-for-us-all

Why I Wear a Hijab

Said, Edward W. *Out of Place: A memoir*. London: Granta, 1999.

The Holy Quran. Translation by A Yusuf Ali. https://quranyusufali.com/

Hijab, Islam and Other Religions

Benhadjoudja, Leila. "Les femmes musulmanes peuvent-elles parler." *Anthropologie et société*, Vol 42, no 1, January 2018.

Lamrabet, Asma. *Women in the Qur'an: An Emancipatory Reading.* Translated by Myriam Francois-Cerrah. London: Square View, 2016.

Mamdani, Mahmood. *Good Muslim, Bad Muslim: America, The Cold War, and the Roots of Terror.* New York: Pantheon, 2004.

The Sublime Quran. Translated by Laleh Bakhtiar. Chicago: Kazi Publications, 2007.

Wadud, Amina. *Qur'an and Woman: Rereading the Sacred Text from a Woman's Perspective.* London: Oxford University Press, 1999.

Growing Up As a Muslim Woman in Tunisia

Béji Ben Mami, Mohamed. "Great Mosque of Zaytuna." In *Discover Islamic Art*, Museum With No Frontiers. 2023. https://islamicart.museumwnf.org/database_item.php?id=monument;isl;tn;mon01;1;en

Ben Salem, Maryam. "Wearing a Veil in Tunisia: From Self-Realization to Passive Resistance." *Revue des Mondes Musulmans et de la Méditerranée* 128, December 2010. https://journals.openedition.org/remmm/6840

Bishku, Michael B. "Kamel Ataturk and Habib Bourguiba: Brothers from different mothers?" In *Kurdish Issues: Essays in Honor of Robert W Olson*, edited by Michael M Gunter, 1-14. Costa Mesa, CA: Mazda Publishers, 2016.

"Habous." *Encyclopedia of the Modern Middle East and North Africa. Encyclopedia.com.* (May 5, 2023). https://www.encyclopedia.com/humanities/encyclopedias-almanacs-transcripts-and-maps/habous

Haddad, Yvonne. "Islamists and the 'Problem of Israel': The 1967 Awakening." *Middle East Journal*, Vol 46, no 2, (Spring 1992): 266-285.

———. "Muhammad Abduh: Pioneer of Islamic Reform." In *Pioneers of Islamic Revival*, 2nd ed, edited by Ali Rahnema. London: Bloomsbury Publishing, 2005.

Husni, Ronak, and Daniel L Newman. *Muslim Women in Law and Society: Annotated translation of al-Tahir al-Haddad's Imra 'tuna fi 'l-sharia wa 'l-mujtama, with an introduction.* London: Routledge, Taylor and Francis Group, 2010.

"Interview with Naama the Lady of Tunisian Song." August 15, 2013. https://www.youtube.com/watch?v=zj84cs9YTDU

Keddie, Nikki R. "Sayyid Jamal al-Din 'al-Afghani." In *Pioneers of Islamic Revival*, 2nd ed, edited by Ali Rahnema. London: Bloomsbury Publishing, 2005.

Macmaster, Neil. *Burning the Veil: The Algerian War and the 'emancipation' of Muslim women, 1954-62.* Manchester: Manchester University Press, 2009.

Mahmood, Saba. *Politics of Piety: The Islamic Revival and the Feminist Subject.* Princeton: Princeton University Press, 2011.

Perkins, Theresa. "Unveiling Muslim Women: The Constitutionality of Hijab Restrictions in Turkey, Tunisia and Kosovo." *Boston University International Law Journal*, Vol 30, (2012): 529-565.

Talbi, Mohamed, L Carl Brown, Emma Murphy, John Innes Clarke and, Nevill Barbour. "Tunisia." *Encyclopedia Britannica.* https://www.britannica.com/place/Tunisia

US Department of State, Office of International Religious Freedom. *2021 Report on International Religious Freedom: Tunisia.* June 2, 2022. https://www.state.gov/reports/2021-report-on-international-religious-freedom/tunisia/

The Innocent Islamophobia

Abu-Lughod, Lila. *Do Muslim Women Need Saving?* Cambridge, MA: Harvard University Press, 2013.

Bahramitash, Roksana. "The War on Terror, Feminist Orientalism and Orientalist Feminism: Case Studies of Two North American Bestsellers." *Critique: Critical Middle Eastern Studies.* Vol 14, no 2, (Summer 2005): 221-235.

Hoodfar, Homa. "The Veil in Their Minds and on Our Heads: Veiling Practices and Muslim Women." In *Women, Gender and Religion: A Reader*, edited by Elizabeth A Castelli. 420-446. New York: Palgrave, 2001.

Mahmoody, Betty and William Hoffer. *Not Without My Daughter.* New York: St Martin's Press, 1987.

Hijab and Employment

Chong, Patricia. "Servitude with a smile: A Re-Examination of Emotional Labour." *Just Labour: A Canadian Journal of Work and Society*, Vol 14, (Autumn 2009): 177-185.

Dooley, Martin D, A Abigail Payne, Leslie Robb. "Understanding the Gaps in Postsecondary Education Participation Based on Income and Place of Birth: The role of high school course selection and performance." Toronto: Higher Education Quality Council of Ontario. 2016.

Henry, Frances, Dua Enakshi, Carl E James, Audrey Kobayashi, Peter Li, Howard Ramos, and Malinda S Smith. "The Equity Myth: Racialization and Indigeneity at Canadian Universities." Vancouver: UBC Press, 2017.

The Canadian Association for University Teachers. "Underrepresented & Underpaid Diversity & Equity Among Canada's Post-Secondary Education Teachers." April 2018. https://www.caut.ca/sites/default/files/caut_equity_report_2018-04final.pdf

Hijab and Public Transit

"1 in 4 Muslim women wearing headscarf shoved on NYC subway: survey." *Daily Sabah.* January 23, 2019. https://www.dailysabah.com/islamophobia/2018/06/21/1-in-4-muslim-women-wearing-headscarf-shoved-on-nyc-subway-survey

Bailey, Moya. https://www.moyabailey.com/

Kahf, Mohja. *Western Representations of the Muslim Woman: From Termagant to Odalisque.* Austin: University of Texas Press, 1999.

Kale, Sirin. "How Islamophobia Hurts Muslim Women the Most." *Vice.* July 2, 2018. https://www.vice.com/en_au/article/nz8pgm/how-islamophobia-hurts-muslim-women-the-most

McPhedran, Taline. "Muslim woman verbally attacked on Ottawa bus thanks driver for intervening." *CTV News.* May 31, 2016. https://www.ctvnews.ca/canada/muslim-woman-verbally-attacked-on-ottawa-bus-thanks-driver-for-intervening-1.2925517

Tumilty, Ryan. "OC Transpo driver who confronted Islamophobia succumbs to cancer." *CBC News.* August 22, 2018. https://www.cbc.ca/news/canada/ottawa/alain-charette-dies-cancer-1.4795269

Hijab and the Media

Bracke, Sarah and LM Hernández Aguilar. "Thinking Europe's 'Muslim Question': On Trojan Horses and the Problematization of Muslims." *Critical Research on Religion*, Vol 10, no 2, (August 2022): 200-220.

Clark, Campbell. "The Bloc's sneaky slur against a mild-mannered Muslim MP." *The Globe and Mail.* January 15, 2021. https://www.theglobeandmail.com/politics/article-the-blocs-sneaky-slur-against-a-mild-mannered-muslim-mp/

Freeman, Joshua. "Family of man fatally stabbed outside Rexdale mosque releases video, says killing should be labelled hate crime." *CTV News.* October 15, 2020. https://toronto.ctvnews.ca/family-of-man-fatally-stabbed-outside-rexdale-mosque-releases-video-says-killing-should-be-labelled-hate-crime-1.5147449

"It's been 6 months since members of the Afzaal family in London, Ont., were killed. What's changed?" *CBC News*. December 6, 2021. https://www.cbc.ca/news/canada/london/it-s-been-6-months-since-members-of-the-afzaal-family-in-london-ont-were-killed-what-s-changed-1.6274751

Jhally, Sut. "Edward Said: on 'Orientalism.'" Media Education Foundation, Challenging Media, released in 2005. https://www.mediaed.org/transcripts/Edward-Said-On-Orientalism-Transcript.pdf

Khan, Mariam. "Muslims are still misrepresented in film and TV, so how do we change the script." *Stylist*. 2021. https://www.stylist.co.uk/entertainment/muslim-representation-film-tv/543599

Legault, Josée. "Sortir des sentiers battus." *Le Journal de Montréal*. January 19, 2021. https://www.pressreader.com/canada/le-journal-de-montreal/20210119/281973200306262

Martineau, Richard. "À quand un chef d'antenne avec un crucifix?" *Le Journal de Montréal*. January, 12, 2021. https://www.pressreader.com/canada/le-journal-de-montreal/20210112/281655372713293

Nawaz, Zarqa. *Little Mosque on the Prairie*. 2007. https://zarqanawaz.com/biography/

Office of the Director of National Intelligence. "Afghan Taliban." Counterterrorism guide. https://www.dni.gov/nctc/groups/afghan_taliban.html

Preston, Alex. "Submission by Michel Houellebecq review—satire that's more subtle than it seems." *The Guardian*. September 8, 2015. https://www.theguardian.com/books/2015/sep/08/submission-michel-houellebecq-review-satire-islamic-france

Ravindran, Manori. "'We Are Lady Parts': Creator Nida Manzoor on Shattering Muslim Stereotypes and Why Representation Isn't a 'Fad.'" *Variety*. June 4, 2021. https://variety.com/2021/tv/global/we-are-lady-parts-linda-lindas-nida-manzoor-1234989061/

Reagan, Ronald. "Photo Op. President Reagan Meeting with Freedom Fighters from Afghanistan (Mujahideen) Oval Office." Presidential Library and Museum. June 16, 1986. https://www.reaganlibrary.gov/archives/video/photo-op-president-reagan-meeting-freedom-fighters-afghanistan-mujahideen-oval

Said, Edward W. *Orientalism*. New York: Pantheon Books, 1978.

Stewart, Emily. "Watch John McCain defend Barack Obama against a racist voter in 2008." *Vox*. Updated September 1, 2018. https://www.vox.com/policy-and-politics/2018/8/25/17782572/john-mccain-barack-obama-statement-2008-video

Watts, Rachel. "6 years later, ceremony held inside Quebec City mosque to honour victims of 2017 attack." *CBC News*. January 29, 2023. https://www.cbc.ca/news/canada/montreal/6-years-later-public-invited-inside-quebec-city-mosque-for-1st-time-since-2017-attack-1.6729050

Zimonjic, Peter. "Trudeau says Bloc leader is using 'coded' language in attack on Transport Minister Omar Alghabra." *CBC News*. January 15, 2021. https://www.cbc.ca/news/politics/omar-alghabra-minister-bloc-blanchet-trudeau-1.5875222

Hijab and Politics

Abedi, Maham. "68% of Canadians want Quebec's face-coverings ban in their province." *Global News*. October 27, 2017. https://globalnews.ca/news/3828752/quebec-face-covering-ban-support-canada-poll/

Bakht, Natasha. *In Your Face: Law, Justice, and Niqab-Wearing Women in Canada*. Toronto: Delve Books, 2020.

Beardsley, Eleanor. "Algeria's 'Black Decade' Still Weighs Heavily." *NPR*. April 25, 2011. https://www.npr.org/2011/04/25/135376589/algerias-black-decade-still-weighs-heavily

"CCPA Analysis Of Bill C-36 An Act To Combat Terrorism." National Office, The Canadian Centre for Policy Alternatives. https://policyalternatives.ca/sites/default/files/uploads/publications/National_Office_Pubs/Terrorism_Act.pdf

Chui, Tina and Hélène Maheux. "Visible Minority Women." *Women in Canada: A Gender-based Statistical Report*, Statistics Canada. July 2011. https://www150.statcan.gc.ca/n1/en/pub/89-503-x/2010001/article/11527-eng.pdf

Ciceri, Coryse. "Le foulard islamique à l'école publique: analyse comparée du débat dans la presse française et québécoise francophone (1994-1995)." mémoire de maîtrise, Université de Montréal, 1998. http://www.metropolis.inrs.ca/medias/wp_05_1998.pdf

Dagenais, Maxime. "Québec Values Charter." *The Canadian Encyclopedia*. February 18, 2014. https://www.thecanadianencyclopedia.ca/en/article/the-charter-of-quebec-values

Dwivedi, Supriya. "Our National Silence on Bill 21." *The Walrus*. October 18, 2019. https://thewalrus.ca/our-national-silence-on-bill-21/

Forcese, Craig and Kent Roach. "Bill C-51: the Good, the Bad . . . and the Truly Ugly." *The Walrus*. February, 13, 2015.

Gagnon, Katia. "Les femmes voilées sont 'manipulées' dit Jeanette Bertrand." *La Presse*. October 16, 2013. https://plus.lapresse.ca/screens/48c9-460c-525d604d-bc14-13e7ac1c6068%7C_0.html

Harris, Kathleen and Alison Crawford Alison. "Federal Court judge under review for berating sex assault complainant." *CBC News*. November 10, 2015. https://www.cbc.ca/news/politics/canada-judge-judical-review-robin-camp-1.3311574

"Hearings on constitutionality of Quebec's secularism law underway in Court of Appeal." *CBC News*. November 7, 2022. https://www.cbc.ca/news/canada/montreal/bill-21-appeal-begins-1.6640434

Journet, Paul. "Charte: Bernard Drainville s'attaque à 'un malaise.'" *La Presse*. September, 11, 2013. https://www.lapresse.ca/actualites/politique/politique-quebecoise/201309/10/01-4688061-charte-bernard-drainville-sattaque-a-un-malaise.php

Kingston, Anne. "Why Stephen Harper doesn't want to talk about 'women's issues.'" *Macleans*. September 11, 2015. https://www.macleans.ca/politics/ottawa/why-stephen-harper-doesnt-want-to-talk-about-womens-issues/

MacCharles, Tonda and Ben Spurr. "Harper pitting country against Muslims, some Niqab wearers say." *The Toronto Star*. October 7, 2015. https://www.thestar.com/news/federal-election/2015/10/07/harper-pitting-country-against-muslims-some-niqab-wearers-say.html

"Marois and Drainville disregard legal advice." *The Globe and Mail*. September 15, 2013. https://www.theglobeandmail.com/opinion/editorials/marois-and-drainville-disregard-legal-advice/article14320723/

Miriam, Chiasson. "The Reasonable Accommodation Crisis, 2007-2008: The Consultation Commission on Accommodation Practices Related to Cultural Differences chaired by Gerard Bouchard and Charles Taylor." For David Howes and the Centaur Jurisprudence Project, The Management of Diversity, Part 2: The Reasonable Accommodation Crisis. Centre for Human Rights and Legal Pluralism, McGill University. August 2012.

Ontario Human Rights Commission–Commission ontarienne des droits de la personne. "Human rights and creed research and consultation report. Section 3: Increase of religion-based hate crime." 2013. https://www.ohrc.on.ca/en/3-current-discrimination-trends/32-underlying-trends-research-and-consultation

Pablo, Carlito. "Vancouver academic deplores assaults against Muslim women amid niqab controversy." *The Georgia Straight*. October 8, 2015. https://www.straight.com/news/553301/vancouver-academic-deplores-assaults-against-muslim-women-amid-niqab-controversy

Patriquin, Martin. "Quebec's sad return to identity politics." *Macleans*. May 31, 2013. https://macleans.ca/general/quebecs-sad-return-to-identity-politics/amp/

Payton, Laura. "For campaign magic, Harper turns to a wizard from Oz." *Macleans*. September 10, 2015. https://macleans.ca/politics/ottawa/for-campaign-magic-harper-turns-to-a-wizard-from-oz/

"Quebec politics 'trapped' by reasonable accommodation debate: Chretien." *The Canadian Press*. October 8, 2018. https://montreal.ctvnews.ca/quebec-politics-trapped-by-reasonable-accommodation-debate-chretien-1.4125397

Radio-Canada. "L'Assemblée nationale adopte le projet de loi sur la neutralité religieuse de l'État." *Radio-Canada*. October 18, 2017. https://ici.radio-canada.ca/nouvelle/1062025/adoption-aujourdhui-projet-loi-neutralite-etat-quebec

Wherry, Aaron. "The niqab ban: 2011-15." *Macleans*. November 16, 2015. https://macleans.ca/politics/ottawa/the-niqab-ban-2011-2015/

Islam, Islamophobia, and Women

American Civil Liberties Union. "Timeline of the Muslim Ban." ACLU Washington, 2017. https://www.aclu-wa.org/pages/timeline-muslim-ban

Association for Canadian Studies–Association d'études Canadiennes. "Law 21: Discourse, Perception & Impacts." ACS Survey, May-June 2022. https://acs-metropolis.ca/wp-content/uploads/2022/08/Report_Survey-Law-21_ACS_Leger-4.pdf

Awan, Imran. "Debunking five social media myths about Muslims and coronavirus." *Middle East Eye*. April 23, 2020. https://www.middleeasteye.net/opinion/coronavirus-muslims-britain-five-social-media-myths

"Black woman wearing hijab threatened at Century Park LRT Station." *CBC News Edmonton*. February 24, 2021. https://www.cbc.ca/news/canada/edmonton/black-woman-wearing-hijab-threatened-at-century-park-lrt-station-1.5926807

Boothby, Lauren. "Third Black Muslim woman attacked in South Edmonton within a week, outside Southgate LRT." *The Edmonton Journal*. December 15, 2020. https://edmontonjournal.com/news/local-news/third-black-muslim-woman-attacked-in-south-edmonton-within-a-week-outside-southgate-lrt

Bruemmer, René. "Muslims the main victims of hate crimes in Montreal this year." *The Montreal Gazette*. June 21, 2019. https://montrealgazette.com/news/local-news/muslims-the-main-victims-of-hate-crimes-in-montreal-this-year

Cox, Ethan. "More Islamophobia in Quebec." *National Post*. February 3, 2014. https://nationalpost.com/opinion/ethan-cox-more-islamophobia-in-quebec

Daro, Ishmael N. "A Toronto Woman Wearing A Niqab Was Attacked In Front Of Her Kids." *BuzzFeed News*. October 6, 2015. https://www.buzzfeed.com/ishmaeldaro/a-toronto-woman-wearing-a-niqab-was-attacked-in-fr

Davey, Jacob, Cécile Guerin and Mackenzie Hart. "An Online Environmental Scan of Right-wing Extremism in Canada." *Institute for Strategic Dialogue*, edited by Jonathan Birdwell. June 19, 2020.

Faucher, Olivier. "Des femmes voilées visées par une série d'incidents haineux à Montréal-Nord." *Le Journal de Montréal*. October 14, 2022. https://www.journaldemontreal.com/2022/10/14/des-femmes-voilees-visees-par-une-serie-dincidents-haineux-a-montreal-nord

Friscolanti, Michael. "Inside the Shafia killings that shocked a nation." *Macleans*. March 3, 2016.

"Hate crimes against Muslims in Canada jump 71 percent." *Middle East Eye*. August 4, 2022. https://www.middleeasteye.net/news/hate-crimes-against-muslims-canada-71-percent

"Hijab-wearing woman attacked in Metro urges others to don religious symbols." *CBC News*. January 13, 2014. https://www.cbc.ca/news/canada/montreal/hijab-wearing-woman-attacked-in-metro-urges-others-to-don-religious-symbols-1.2494575

Huncar, Andrea. "Far-right extremists getting bolder as threatening behaviour goes unchecked, police warned." *CBC News Edmonton*. May 11, 2020. https://www.cbc.ca/news/canada/edmonton/ramadan-bombathon-edmonton-mosque-far-right-extremists-police-charges-1.5564323

Kestler-D'Amours, Jillian. "Why are Muslim women living 'in fear' in this Canadian city?" *Al Jazeera*. July 13, 2021. https://www.aljazeera.com/news/2021/7/13/why-are-muslim-women-living-in-fear-in-this-canadian-city

Kohut, Tania. "Zunera Ishaq takes citizenship oath wearing niqab after challenging ban." *Global News*. October 9, 2015. https://globalnews.ca/news/2269064/zunera-ishaq-takes-citizenship-oath-wearing-niqab-after-challenging-ban/

Lachacz, Adam. "'She was thrown to the ground': Police investigate attack on Muslim woman in Edmonton." *CTV News Edmonton*. June 13, 2021. https://edmonton.ctvnews.ca/she-was-thrown-to-the-ground-police-investigate-attack-on-muslim-woman-in-edmonton-1.5468914

Lau, Rachel. "Montreal woman says man tried to rip off her niqab, attackers now have 'no age, gender or colour.'" *Global News*. May 15, 2019. https://globalnews.ca/news/5279410/woman-with-niqab-claims-attack-charlevoix-metro/

Mertz, Emily. "St. Albert RCMP look for suspect after woman grabbed by hijab, knocked unconscious." *Global News*. June 24, 2021. https://globalnews.ca/news/7977887/st-albert-rcmp-look-for-suspect-after-woman-grabbed-by-hijab-knocked-unconscious/

Mirza, Heidi Safia. "Embodying the Veil: Muslim Women and Gendered Islamophobia in 'New Times.'" In *Gender, Religion and Education in a Chaotic Postmodern World*, (January 2013): 303-316. https://www.researchgate.net/publication/301955536_Embodying_the_Veil_Muslim_Women_and_Gendered_Islamophobia_in_'New_Times', August 2013.

Montpetit, Jonathan. "Muslim women report spike in harassment, discrimination since Bill 21 tabled." *CBC News*. May 13, 2019. https://www.cbc.ca/news/canada/montreal/muslim-women-report-spike-in-harassment-discrimination-since-bill-21-tabled-1.5134539

"Montreal Metro scarf tangling leads to woman's death." *CBC News*. January 31, 2014. https://www.cbc.ca/news/canada/montreal/montreal-metro-scarf-tangling-leads-to-woman-s-death-1.2516971

Moreau, Greg. "Police-reported hate crime in Canada, 2018." *Juristat*, Statistics Canada. February 26, 2020. https://www150.statcan.gc.ca/n1/pub/85-002-x/2020001/article/00003-eng.htm

"Quebec Muslim Badia Senouci told: 'change your religion.'" *CBC News*. September 16, 2013. https://www.cbc.ca/news/canada/montreal/quebec-muslim-badia-senouci-told-change-your-religion-1.1855675

Raza, Ali. "Anti-Muslim hate 'normalized' for too long, say many in Muslim community mourning deadly London attack." *CBC News Toronto*. June 8, 2021. https://www.cbc.ca/news/canada/toronto/london-attack-islamophobia-1.6058161

Rukavina, Steve. "New research shows Bill 21 having 'devastating' impact on religious minorities in Quebec." *CBC News*. August 4, 2022. https://www.cbc.ca/news/canada/montreal/bill-21-impact-religious-minorities-survey-1.6541241

Slater, Joanna and Niha Masih. "As the world looks for coronavirus scapegoats, Muslims are blamed in India." *The Washington Post*. April 23, 2020.

Snowdon, Wallis. "Woman in hijab assaulted in 2nd 'hate-motivated' attack in Edmonton this month." *CBC News Edmonton*. December 16, 2020. https://www.cbc.ca/news/canada/edmonton/southgate-lrt-assault-hijab-hate-motivated-1.5813642

Wang, Jing Hui, and Greg Moreau. "Police-reported hate crime in Canada, 2020." *Juristat*, Statistics Canada. March 17, 2022. https://www150.statcan.gc.ca/n1/pub/85-002-x/2022001/article/00005-eng.htm

Zine, Jasmine. "Unveiled Sentiments: Gendered Islamophobia and Experiences of Veiling among Muslim Girls in a Canadian Islamic School, Equity and Excellence in Education." Vol 39, no 3, (September 2006): 239-252. https://www.researchgate.net/publication/248929877_Unveiled_Sentiments_Gendered_Islamophobia_and_Experiences_of_Veiling_among_Muslim_Girls_in_a_Canadian_Islamic_School

The Multiple Layers of Hate

Abu-Lughod, Lila. *Do Muslim Women Need Saving?* Cambridge, MA: Harvard University Press, 2013.

"Afghan Activist: George W Bush's Claim US War in Afghanistan Protected Women Is a 'Shameless Lie.'" *Democracy Now*. Jul 15 2021. https://www.democracynow.org/2021/7/15/afghanistan_taliban_us_withdrawal

Ahmed, Leila. *The Quiet Revolution: The Veil's Resurgence, from the Middle East to America*. New Haven, CT: Yale University Press, 2011.

Allen, Mike. "Bush Reverses Abortion Aid." *The Washington Post*. January 23, 2001. https://www.washingtonpost.com/archive/politics/2001/01/23/bush-reverses-abortion-aid/7439b0dc-d105-459d-bcf2-a8f82f076082/

Berry, Kim. "The Symbolic Use of Afghan Women in the war on terror." *Humboldt Journal of Social Relations*, Vol 27, no 2 (2003): 137-160.

"Bush declares National Sanctity of Human Life Day." *CNN News*. January 15, 2003. https://www.cnn.com/2003/ALLPOLITICS/01/15/bush.abortion/index.html

"George Bush says Afghan girls will suffer 'unspeakable harm' after US withdrawal." *The National News*. July 14, 2021. https://www.thenationalnews.com/world/us-news/2021/07/14/george-bush-says-afghan-girls-will-suffer-unspeakable-harm-after-us-withdrawal/

Rizvi, Rania. "Internalized Islamophobia: 9/11's insidious aftermath." *The Daily Targum*, Cornell University. December 9, 2020. https://dailytargum.com/article/2020/12/internalized-islamophobia-9-11s-insidious-aftermath

Systemic Islamophobia or A Few Bad Apples?

Arnold, Steve. "Hamilton rabbis express horror at killing of Muslim family in London." *The Hamilton Jewish News*. June 11, 2021. https://www.hamiltonjewishnews.com/news/hamilton-rabbis-express-horror-at-killing-of-muslim-family-in-london

Beaumont, Hilary. "Imams in Canada express solidarity with Indigenous people." *Al Jazeera*. July 9, 2021. https://www.aljazeera.com/news/2021/7/9/imams-in-canada-express-solidarity-with-indigenous-people

Boutilier, Alex. "Liberal MP swamped by hate mail, threats over anti-Islamophobia motion in Commons." *The Toronto Star*. February 16, 2017. https://www.thestar.com/news/canada/2017/02/16/liberal-mp-swamped-by-hate-mail-threats-over-anti-islamophobia-motion-in-commons.html

———. "Rise of right-wing extremists presents new challenge for Canadian law enforcement agencies." *The Toronto Star*. October 7, 2018. https://www.thestar.com/news/canada/2018/10/07/rise-of-right-wing-extremists-presents-new-challenge-for-canadian-law-enforcement-agencies.html

Canada, Parliament, House of Commons. "M-103 Systemic Racism and religious discrimination." 42nd Parliament, 1st Session. March 23, 2017. https://www.ourcommons.ca/members/en/88849/motions/8661986

———. "Taking action against Systemic Racism and Religious Discrimination Including Islamophobia." Report of the Standing Committee on Canadian Heritage, 42nd Parliament, 1st session. February 2018. https://www.ourcommons.ca/Content/Committee/421/CHPC/Reports/RP9315686/chpcrp10/chpcrp10-e.pdf

Djuric, Mickey. "Canada's new anti-Islamophobia representative apologizes for comments about Quebecers." *CTV News*. February 1, 2023.

Draaisma, Muriel. "Toronto mosque launches food drive in honour of volunteer caretaker killed 1 year ago." *CBC News*. September 12, 2021. https://www.cbc.ca/news/canada/toronto/etobicoke-mosque-killing-volunteer-caretaker-food-drive-1.6173279

Elghawaby, Amira. "Canada is Holding an Emergency Summit to Take Action Against Islamophobia. Here's What's at Stake for Canadian Muslims." *PressProgress*. July 19, 2021.

Loreto, Nora. "Why François Legault is wrong about Islamophobia in Quebec." *Canada's National Observer*. February 13, 2019. https://www.nationalobserver.com/2019/02/13/opinion/why-francois-legault-wrong-about-islamophobia-quebec

"Man charged in death of Etobicoke mosque caretaker found not criminally responsible." *The Canadian Press*. March 27, 2023. https://www.cbc.ca/news/canada/toronto/mosque-stabbing-not-criminally-responsible-1.6792418

"Man charged in stabbing death of Etobicoke mosque caretaker." *CBC News*. September 18, 2020. https://www.cbc.ca/news/canada/toronto/man-charged-death-mosque-caretaker-1.5730329

"Man charged in stabbing death of mosque caretaker followed hate group online." *CBC News*. September 21, 2020. https://www.cbc.ca/news/canada/toronto/mosque-stabbing-suspect-1.5732078

McCooey, Paula. "Federal funding helps increase security at Muslim places of worship." *The Ottawa Citizen*. November 27, 2017. https://ottawacitizen.com/news/local-news/federal-funding-helps-to-protect-muslim-community

Miller, Christopher. "Canada Has Added More US Far-Right Extremists To Its List Of Banned Terrorists." *BuzzFeed News*. June 25, 2021. https://www.buzzfeednews.com/article/christopherm51/canada-terror-three-percenters

"Muslim family in Canada killed in 'premeditated' truck attack." *BBC News*. June 8, 2021. https://www.bbc.com/news/world-us-canada-57390398

Perry, Barbara and Ryan Scrivens. "Uneasy Alliances: A Look at the Right-Wing Extremist Movement in Canada." *Studies in Conflict & Terrorism*, Vol 39, no 9 (2016): 819-841, September 15, 2015.

"Quebec doesn't have a problem with Islamophobia, Premier Legault says." *CBC News*. January 31, 2019. https://www.cbc.ca/news/canada/montreal/quebec-mosque-shooting-islamophobia-1.5000950

"The Government of Canada Concludes National Summit on Islamophobia." Government of Canada–Le gouvernement du Canada. July 22, 2023.

Colonialism and Women

"Canada Stolen Sisters: A Human Rights Response to Discrimination and Violence against Indigenous Women in Canada." Amnesty International, Canada, 2004. https://www.amnesty.ca/sites/amnesty/files/amr200032004enstolensisters.pdf

"Colonising Algeria was crime against humanity, Macron." *The Morning Call, Africa News*. February 17, 2017. https://www.youtube.com/watch?v=nvV43ICfMWE

Crabb, Josh. "Canadians need to understand impacts of colonization, MMIWG advocate says." *CTV News Winnipeg*. September 29, 2021. https://winnipeg.ctvnews.ca/canadians-need-to-understand-impacts-of-colonization-mmiwg-advocate-says-1.5605936

Earl of Cromer, *Modern Egypt*, 2 vols. New York: Macmillan, 1908.

Fanon, Frantz. "Algeria Unveiled." In *Decolonization Perspectives from Now and Then*, edited by Prasanjit Duara. 42-55. London: Routledge, Taylor and Francis Group, 2003. https://academics.skidmore.edu/blogs/transnational-s19/files/2014/08/Fanon-Algeria-Unveiled.pdf

"France's Macron No Repentance Nor Apologies for Algeria Occupation During Independence War." *VOA News*. January 20, 2021. https://www.voanews.com/a/europe_france macron-no-repentance-nor-apologies-algeria-occupation-during-independence-war/6200981.html

Kebsi, Jyhene. "Unveil Them to Save Them: France and the Ongoing Colonization of Muslim Women's Bodies." Georgetown University, Berkley Centre for Religion, Peace and World Affairs. May 13, 2021. https://berkleycenter.georgetown.edu/responses/unveil-them-to-save-them-france-and-the-ongoing-colonization-of-muslim-women-s-bodies

Kennedy, Mark. "'Simply a savage': How the residential schools came to be." *The Ottawa Citizen*. May 22, 2015. https://ottawacitizen.com/news/politics/simply-a-savage-how-the-residential-schools-came-to-be

Lamrabet, Asma. "Muslim Women's Veil, Between the colonial ideology and traditionalist Islamic ideology: a decolonized vision." http://www.asma-lamrabet.com/articles/muslim-women-s-veil-between-the-colonial-ideology-and-traditionalist-islamic-ideology-a-decolonized-vision/

"Missing and Murdered Aboriginal Women: A National Operational Overview." Royal Canadian Mounted Police–La Gendarmerie royale du Canada, 2014. https://www.rcmp-grc.gc.ca/en/missing-and-murdered-aboriginal-women-national-operational-overview#sec3

Rahal, Malika. "Algeria: Nonviolent resistance against French colonialism, 1830s-1950s." Edited by Maciej J Bartkowski. Rienner, pp.107-223, 2013. ffhal-01316088

"Reclaiming Power and Place: The Final Report of the National Inquiry into Missing and Murdered Indigenous Women and Girls." National Inquiry into missing and murdered Indigenous women and girls, 2019. https://www.mmiwg-ffada.ca/

"Truth and Reconciliation Commission of Canada." Government of Canada–Gouvernement du Canada, 2015. https://www.rcaanc-cirnac.gc.ca/eng/1450124405592/1529106060525#chp2

Hijabization As Fashion

Alleyne, Allyssia. "Dolce & Gabbana debuts line of hijabs and abayas." *CNN News*. August 26, 2016. https://www.cnn.com/style/article/dolce-gabbana-muslim-hijab-abaya/index.html

Bucar, Liz. "Three things we can learn from contemporary Muslim women's fashion." *The Conversation*. November 5, 2018. https://theconversation.com/three-things-we-can-learn-from-contemporary-muslim-womens-fashion-104889

Kingsley, Patrick. "Egypt criminalises sexual harassment for first time." *The Guardian*. June 6, 2014. https://www.theguardian.com/world/2014/jun/06/egypt-criminalises-sexual-harassment

Ray, Michael. "Amr Khaled: Egyptian Televangelist." *Encyclopedia Britannica*. https://www.britannica.com/biography/Amr-Khaled

"Sexual Harassment and Domestic Violence in the Middle East and North." *Arab Barometer*. December 2019. https://www.arabbarometer.org/wp-content/uploads/Sexual-Harassement-Domestic-Violence-Arab-Citizens-Public-Opinion-2019.pdf

Hijabi Trends

Ghanem, Khaoula. "Dina Tokio Responds to Trolls by Reading Out Their Most Horrific Comments." *Vogue Arabia*. January 6, 2019. https://en.vogue.me/culture/dina-tokio-responds-to-trolls-by-reading-out-their-most-horrific-comments/

Montpetit, Jonathan. "What we can learn from Hérouxville, the Quebec town that became shorthand for intolerance." *CBC News*. January 25, 2017. https://www.cbc.ca/news/canada/montreal/herouxville-quebec-reasonable-accommodation-1.3950390

Islam and Feminism

Abu-Lughod, Lila. *Do Muslim Women Need Saving?* Cambridge, MA: Harvard University Press, 2013.

Mir-Hosseini, Ziba. "Beyond 'Islam' vs 'Feminism.'" *Institute of Development Studies*, Vol 42, no 1, (January 2011).

Musawah for Equality in the Family. https://www.musawah.org/

Sisters in Islam. https://sistersinislam.org/

Privilege and Solidarity

Light, Alison. *Mrs Woolf and the Servants: An Intimate History of Domestic Life in Bloomsbury*. London: Bloomsbury Publishing, 2008.

Sandberg, Sheryl. *Lean In: Women, Work, and the Will to Lead*. New York: Knopf, 2013.

Yacoubi, Imen. "Sovereignty from below: State Feminism and Politics of Women against Women in Tunisia." *The Arab Studies Journal*, Vol 24, no 1, (Spring 2016): 254-274.

The Evolving Hijab

Haydar, Mona. "Hijabi Wrap my hijab." April 1, 2017. https://www.youtube.com/watch?v=NoFWEAevIuQ

Conclusion

Canada, Parliament, House of Commons. "Mauril Bélanger on Canadian Islamic History Month." 39th Parliament, 2nd session. October 25, 2007. https://www.ourcommons.ca/DocumentViewer/en/39-2/house/sitting-8/hansard#OOB-2179382